An Examination
of Problems and Opportunities
Facing a City

FAITH IN THE CITY
OF BIRMINGHAM

The Report of a Commission set up by
the Bishop's Council of the Diocese of Birmingham

CHAIRMAN : SIR RICHARD O'BRIEN

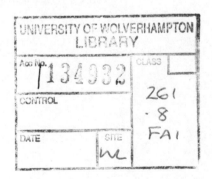
Exeter
The Paternoster Press

AUSTRALIA:
Bookhouse Australia Ltd.,
P.O. Box 115, Flemington Markets, NSW 2129

SOUTH AFRICA:
Oxford University Press,
P.O. Box 1141, Cape Town

British Library Cataloguing in Publication Data

Faith in the city of Birmingham: an
examination of problems and opportunities
facing the city: the report of a
commission set up by the Bishop's Council
of the Diocese of Birmingham.
1. Great Britain. Urban regions. Christian church
274.1

ISBN 0–85364–474–8

Typeset in Great Britain by
Photoprint, 9–11 Alexandra Lane, Torquay, Devon
and printed for The Paternoster Press,
Paternoster House, 3 Mount Radford Crescent, Exeter, Devon
by A. Wheaton & Co. Ltd., Exeter, Devon.

PREFACE

TO: **Rt. Revd. Mark Santer, Bishop of Birmingham**

The Commission entitled FAITH IN THE CITY OF BIRMINGHAM was set up by the Bishop's Council of the Diocese of Birmingham on the initiative of your predecessor, Bishop Hugh Montefiore, after consultation with the other Presidents of the Birmingham Council of Christian Churches. We were charged 'to examine and report upon the social and economic problems and opportunities facing the City of Birmingham together with the problems and opportunities which face its Churches'. This we have now done and our report is submitted to you. It is unanimous.

We have held 12 Commission meetings and have attempted to address the whole of urban life in Birmingham with particular reference to Urban Priority Areas. Our discussions have been greatly assisted by the evidence we received from many groups and individuals and from the visits which we made to see and hear at first hand from those involved in Urban Priority Areas. To all whom we met and who wrote to us we express our thanks and appreciation; their names are listed in Appendix A.

The project has received financial support from the following organizations: the Barrow and Geraldine Cadbury Trust; Birmingham Diocesan Board of Finance; Copec Housing Trust; the Gulbenkian Foundation and the Wates Foundation. We thank them all for their support which has made our work possible.

We owe a particular debt of gratitude to the City Council which not only made a grant towards our administrative expenses but also loaned us the services of Mr. Alan Tolley. He performed his tasks as Administrative Officer with admirable zeal and competence and we are grateful to him.

We are greatly indebted to Mr. Kenneth Spencer, our Research Officer. He has worked tirelessly on sifting and collating the evidence and on preparing draft chapters for our consideration. His equanimity, good humour and professionalism have been appreciated by us all. It is to him we owe the completion of the report within the time specified in our terms of reference.

We have learned much from our task. Our faith in the future of Birmingham has been confirmed and strengthened. We hope that our report will be of value to you and your colleagues in the Church of England and in other churches. We hope too that civic and other leaders will find it of service as they go about their business of guiding Birmingham into the 1990s and beyond. We extend to you and to them our confident good wishes.

25th March 1988
RICHARD O'BRIEN

MEMBERS OF THE COMMISSION

Chairman
Sir Richard O'Brien — Chairman, Policy Studies Institute, formerly Chairman of A.C.C.U.P.A.

Vice Chairman
The Venerable John Duncan — Archdeacon of Birmingham

Members

Professor Gordon Cherry	Professor of Urban & Regional Planning, Birmingham University
Ken Cure	Executive Council Member, A.E.U.W.
Keith Dennis	Headteacher, Shenley Court Comprehensive School
Monsignor Tom Fallon	Parish Priest, Handsworth
Reverend John Haslam	Solicitor and non-stipendiary priest
Peter Houghton	Director, Birmingham Settlement
Dr. Mary Jeavons	G.P., Chelmsley Wood
Reverend Les. Milner	Director, St. Basil's Centre
Rt. Reverend Lesslie Newbigin	Theologian and Minister, Winson Green
Reverend Desmond Pemberton	Wesleyan Holiness Church
Professor John M. Samuels	Professor of Business Finance, Department of Accounting, Birmingham University
Dr. John Sawkill	Director, Tube Investments
James Wilson	General Manager, Bournville Village Trust
Hazel Wright	Headteacher, Grove Infant and Nursery School, Grove Lane, Handsworth

Consultant

Graham Shaylor   Director of Development,
                                                 Birmingham City Council

Observer

Ultan Russell   Executive Secretary, Birmingham
                                                 Council of Christian Churches

Officers

Kenneth Spencer   Institute of Local Government
                                                 Studies, Birmingham University
Alan Tolley   Senior Administrative Officer,
                                                 Birmingham City Council

GROUP MEMBERS WHO PRODUCED PART IV, CHAPTER 6
OF THE REPORT, "CHRISTIAN PRESPECTIVES ON THE CITY"

Bishop Lesslie Newbigin   Dr. David Ford
Father Ron Darwin SJ   Reverend K. E. Gray
                    Reverend Renate Wilkinson

CONTENTS

PART II   CHRISTIAN RESPONSES

PART I

Birmingham in Perspective

Chapter One

INTRODUCTION

1.1   'Faith in the City', the Report of the Archbishop of Canterbury's Commission on Urban Priority Areas, was published in 1985. Since that time the Churches and others, in Birmingham and elsewhere, have been considering ways in which they should respond in order to play their part in improving the quality of life, spiritually and materially, in these areas. 'Faith in the City' was concerned with the whole of England; this Report is about Birmingham — a city which the Archbishop's Commission confirmed as possessing one of the highest percentages of deprived districts in the country. Over one million people live in the City. Many possess resources which enable them to live full and even prosperous lives, with optimism and hope for the future. Others have few resources and suffer from a sense of powerlessness and exclusion. The Commission's hope is that *all* citizens of Birmingham will share in the benefits of economic growth.

1.2   'Faith in the City' defined Urban Priority Areas in these terms: 'What we now call urban priority areas are districts of specially disadvantaged character. They are places which suffer from economic decline, physical decay, and social disintegration. These factors interlock and together they describe multiple and relative deprivation . . . Such is the UPA, constituting a different Britain, whose people are prevented from entering fully into the mainstream of the normal life of the nation . . .'

1.3   We believe that the situation in Birmingham demands a considered and sustained response. The Commission has been impressed by the ready acknowledgement of the problems by the City authorities and others and by the efforts and the resources which are already mobilized to alleviate and to change the condition of the disadvantaged. Nevertheless an unacceptable level of deprivation continues to persist. We have found that there is a tendency for the deprived and the disadvantaged to be left behind in Urban Priority

Areas and for the successful to move out. These areas are to be found both within the inner city and on the large peripheral housing estates.

Identifying Urban Priority Areas

1.4   The Department of the Environment used 1981 census data to identify these areas, using the following information:
   (a) unemployment
   (b) old people living alone
   (c) single-parent families
   (d) ethnicity — the proportion of people in households whose head was born in the New Commonwealth or Pakistan
   (e) overcrowding of dwellings
   (f) dwellings lacking basic amenities

1.5   'Faith in the City' concluded that on a diocesan basis the heaviest concentration of Urban Priority Areas in England and Wales was in the Diocese of Birmingham. Birmingham also heads the list of local authorities with the highest number of deprived census enumeration districts, having 677 of the 'most deprived' ten per cent of enumeration districts in England and Wales. Of these 470 were in the Inner City Core Area (as defined by the Birmingham Inner City Partnership) with the remaining 207 in the rest of the City. Ten per cent of enumeration districts nationally were defined by the Department of the Environment as 'most deprived' but the figure for Birmingham was 32 per cent, almost a third of the City. Within the Inner City Core Area itself 83 per cent of enumeration districts were in the 'most deprived' category.

1.6   The criteria used to identify Urban Priority Areas result in a tendency to identify older areas of housing as Urban Priority Areas rather than more recent developments. It is important for local knowledge and judgement to play its part in decisions about defining Urban Priority Areas. In the light of this the Church of England Diocese of Birmingham has carried out its own exercise on classifying Urban Priority Area parishes. This shows that of its 183 diocesan parishes (containing 1.42 million people as the diocese extends beyond the City boundary), 57 (containing 450,000 people) fall within the Urban Priority Area definition, with at least six enumeration districts per parish being within the worst ten per cent nationally. Another 20 parishes were added on the basis of local knowledge and judgement — thus 77 parishes, or 42 per cent, were considered to be

Urban Priority Areas (containing a population of about 703,000 people) in the Diocese of Birmingham.

1.7   Map 1.1 (p. 157) shows the distribution of enumeration districts falling into the 'most deprived' 10 per cent of enumeration districts nationally. The main concentration is in the core inner city area. The electoral wards of the City with the highest concentrations of 'most deprived' enumeration districts are Sparkbrook, Small Heath and Sparkhill, Soho, Handsworth, Aston and Sandwell, Washwood Heath and Nechells and parts of Edgbaston. Of the outer areas, Kingstanding, Stockland Green, Acocks Green, Billesley and Longbridge have significant numbers of enumeration districts among the 'most deprived' nationally. At the other extreme Sutton Four Oaks, Sutton Vesey, Sutton New Hall, Perry Barr, Sheldon, Bartley Green, Northfield, Kings Norton, Bournville, Quinton, Harborne, Selly Oak, Hall Green, and Shard End have none or very few deprived enumeration districts. Map 1.2 (p. 158) indicates electoral ward areas, the Inner City Partnership Area, the Inner City Core Area, and the Priority Ring (agreed in November 1982).

The Urban Priority Areas of Birmingham

1.8   Urban Priority Areas are parts of the City with the worst concentrations of urban deprivation. Many suffer from what is called multiple deprivation. Unemployment levels are high; housing conditions are deteriorating; crime rates are above average; incomes are lower and many are dependent on state welfare benefits. There is often a high incidence of single parent families and of old people living alone. Educational performance and health standards are generally lower than the average. These factors are often aggravated by racial prejudice. The Birmingham economy is now beginning to recover, but those who live in Urban Priority Areas are not sharing in the economic gains.

The Commission's Method

1.9   In addition to individual Commission members, the research officer and the Anglican Diocese of Birmingham, who provided material, other bodies were approached with requests to submit evidence. Press advertisements were placed seeking public response, and members of the Commission undertook a series of visits to meet residents and those working in the Urban Priority Areas.

1.10   In this Report, we have sought to voice our concern about the situation within these deprived areas. We have tried to take into account the spiritual and material needs of the whole person. It has not been our intention to provide a blueprint for action. What we have endeavoured to do is to open a window on Urban Priority. Area life within the City in the late 1980s. We hope the people who read our Report will develop their own actions arising out of it. The conclusions and recommendations are designed to provide help and guidance. We are confident of a response. Birmingham is a proud city with a strong municipal tradition of commitment to action on behalf of all its citizens including the deprived and the disadvantaged. This response needs to come from all sectors — public, private and voluntary — and from many individuals if it is to be successful.

Chapter Two

A SHORT HISTORY OF BIRMINGHAM

Introduction

2.1 This brief history presents some of the elements which have shaped Birmingham and especially the Urban Priority Areas. The ability of the City to respond to challenges is determined not only by the hope and vision of the future, but also by its past and by the nature of its inheritance.

2.2 Cities grow because of economic activity. The lifeblood of Birmingham has been its industry — the industrial heartland of England. Industrialization and its impact upon the lives of residents provides the core of this history. Yet history is also about social patterns, especially those concerning housing and migration which help to explain the nature of life within the City. Attention is also focused upon the evolution of social disparities within the City, and upon the present pattern of Urban Priority Areas.

2.3 Chapter 1 has dealt with the definition of Urban Priority Areas within Birmingham. Such areas need to be placed in historical perspective. They reflect past decisions and are creatures of the whole of our urban and national society — not the creations of their residents.

The Emerging City up to 1918

2.4 The West Midlands has traditionally been seen as a prosperous, buoyant region able to adapt to industrial change. Its prosperity was founded upon the industries associated with coal, steel and metalworking. Birmingham has the advantage of a central position in relation to the successive transport networks of canal, railway and motorway, and has developed as a finishing centre to meet the growing demands of national and international markets for

7

metal goods. Coal, limestone and iron were readily available nearby. Birmingham was able to complement these natural resources with enterprise, initiative and skill, related to:

(a) a well-developed credit structure which enabled 'masters' to oversee the production process by arranging orders and payments to the many, often small, specialized firms, engaged in the various stages of manufacturing processes;

(b) the ability of entrepreneurs to seize opportunities to develop new or expanded markets and organize the flow of materials, skill and capital necessary to take advantage of such markets;

(c) the lack of a restrictive Guild tradition in Birmingham encouraged a higher degree of inventiveness and innovation;

(d) the existence of skilled and highly specialized labour which quickly developed across a host of metal-working activities;

(e) the ability to be adaptable and flexible in meeting new fashions, new markets, and innovating product development and design.

2.5　　From the seventeenth century the Birmingham economy progressively developed more complex metal goods. Thus to the manufacture of jewellery, guns, metal buttons, buckles and brassware of the early nineteenth century were added hinges, edge tools, grates, fire irons, fenders and light iron castings. By 1860 Birmingham and the Black Country were the centre of UK hardware production. Later the development of specialist engineering industries proceeded at an accelerated pace enabling a rapid growth in manufacture of bicycles, motor bikes, motor vehicles and electrical goods. These all had a host of component firms supplying the main manufacturers.

2.6　　The provision of finance and trading services grew. Manufacturers' associations developed as markets expanded. By 1849, of the eight leading banks in the City, six were Birmingham owned and managed. Improved rail services led to the development of regional shopping facilities in the 1860s and 1870s.

2.7　　Birmingham's industrial base changed when the Black Country's reserves of coal, limestone and iron became depleted. New processes meant that steel replaced iron, leading to decline in the old iron hardware trades in the last decades of the nineteenth century and the rise of tools, brassware, bolts, screws, tubes.

2.8　　By 1914 Birmingham's growth industries were light and medium engineering, particularly the manufacture of cycles, motor vehicles, and, to a lesser degree, electrical equipment. Industries which exploited the advance of automated methods, introduced on the basis of cheap steel and using local skilled metal workers and the wide range of component part industries, prospered.

2.9   It was the motor vehicle industry (led by Herbert Austin) which made Birmingham an important centre of motor manufacture between the early 1900s and the First World War. That war rescued the Birmingham economy from the stagnation which had threatened it up to the turn of the century, bringing orders for munitions, vehicles, tanks and spare parts. It also speeded up the adoption of mechanized and standardized factory processes. The abrupt termination of war-time orders, however, produced slump conditions and the sudden exposure of uncompetitive industries and firms.

2.10   From the latter part of the nineteenth century Birmingham manufacturers had to meet increasing international competition from other rapidly industrializing nations, especially Germany, France, the USA and Japan. This had led to pressure for trade tariff reform to protect the City's industries from the impact of overseas competition and trade cycle fluctuations. That part of the workforce which tended to be employed in prosperous times and unemployed in depressions were the most vulnerable. They often lived in overcrowded, poor, nineteenth century rented dwellings in the older central housing areas of the City. These were the nineteenth century Urban Priority Areas.

2.11   The cultural history of the City was widely reflected in its politics. Birmingham's distinctive social and economic structure strongly shaped its politics. The absence of a landed class and the many small masters made it a radical city in the early nineteenth century. Its small scale industries and high social mobility stopped the emergence of class struggle between employers and employed.

2.12   Rapid industrial expansion meant increasing population. The 71,000 residents of the City in 1801 had grown to 401,000 by 1881 and just over 1 million by 1931. In the nineteenth century people moved to the City from surrounding rural and urban areas and there was a large influx of Irish migrants in the mid nineteenth century. The population grew especially after 1911. Between 1891 and 1911 the central area of the City lost population as the suburbs expanded and the population moved out to make way for commercial development, new roads and slum clearance. It was usually the nineteenth century Urban

Priority Area dweller who was displaced by this development of the City. Displacement usually spilled over to nearby old decaying residential property. Thus what we would regard as Urban Priority Areas have never been static.

Municipal Achievements

2.13   In the 1870s and early 1880s Birmingham gained an international reputation as being the best governed city in the world. Civic pride was the driving force of a new civic philosophy, known at that time and since as 'the civic gospel'. Birmingham was regarded as experimental, adventurous and diverse. This set a tradition in Birmingham of leadership in municipal enterprise. This period also saw a strong tradition of co-operation between middle and working class groups. The social character of the city was reflected, in contrast to other cities, by greater diversity of occupations; work done in small workshops rather than factories; a high proportion of the labour force being skilled; considerable social mobility.

2.14   It was Nonconformist ministers who first proclaimed the civic gospel. George Dawson was particularly prominent from 1844–1876. His congregations included many influential people in civic life. His common purpose was to stress the importance of policies for the benefit of all the people and that religion was to be judged by its effects on practical conduct.

2.15   Other significant Nonconformist ministers included Charles Vince and H. W. Crosskey (Chamberlain was a member of his congregation). Robert Dale (pastor of Carrs Lane Congregational Church 1854–1895) was especially influential. Indeed, Carrs Lane became known as the centre of Nonconformity. A prominent industrialist, George Muntz, said of Dale: 'I never see Dale rising without thinking of the Church militant.' Dale had a strong conviction that those who declined to use their political power were guilty of treachery both to God and man. By comparison, in the late nineteenth century Methodism was relatively weak in Birmingham, and the Anglican and Roman Catholic churches played little part in local politics. In Chapter 3 we shall develop many of these points further.

2.16   Chamberlain's period as Mayor from 1873–76 saw the implementation of a civic gospel with origins not only in the economic and social alliances but in religious idealism and growing dissatisfaction with narrow views of the role of local government. From this period slums were cleared, Corporation Street was constructed, the gas and water services were municipalized, the high city death rate reduced.

2.17   Prosperity was not enjoyed by all. In the poorer districts close to the town centre housing was grossly unhealthy and overcrowded. As part of the new municipal enterprise the slum area was demolished to build Corporation Street but those displaced were not adequately rehoused. A description of the housing conditions for poor families in the 1880s was given by the Medical Officer of Health: '. . . narrow streets, houses without back doors or windows, situated both in and out of courts; confined yards; courts open at one end only, and others with small and narrow openings; the impossibility in many instances of providing sufficient privy accommodation; houses and shopping so dilapidated as to be in imminent danger of falling, and incapable of proper repair'; there was, he continued, 'want of ventilation, want of light, want of proper and decent accommodation', and 'the dreary desolation acre after acre at the very heart of the town'.

2.18   Bad health, high infant mortality, insanitary and overcrowded housing reflected the disparities between the poor and more prosperous areas of the City. That disparity, in different forms, remains to this day. Over time the structure of urban problems has changed, but Urban Priority Areas survive.

The Inter-War Years

2.19   After 1918 Birmingham manufacture increasingly concentrated on the motor industry and its associated components. Interdependence between firms was developed especially in the 1920s and 1930s. Other companies moved into the City e.g. Dunlop from Dublin (rubber tyres) and Lucas (electrical components), while others expanded production. After 1915 motor vehicle manufacture was protected by the McKenna duty on imported cars and parts. The British-owned car industry was based in the Midlands and rationalizations and acquisitions began concentrating manufacture in fewer companies. Amalgamations meant a growth in the size of production units. This trend accelerated after the Second World War. BSA, which had moved into bicycles, and later motor bikes when the gun trade was depressed in the 1880s, began to buy companies in other towns e.g. Daimler in Coventry in 1910. Cadburys merged with Frys of Bristol in 1919 and retained their role not only as employers but as local benefactors conscious of the wider welfare of Birmingham citizens as the Bournville Village Trust exemplifies. Many city firms were incorporated into the huge Tube Investments company, while the munitions firm of G. Kynoch was taken over by ICI. BSA amalgamated with Lanchester in the 1930s, Morris took over Wolseley Motors in 1927. Some firms retained their strong local base and expanded, while others were absorbed by firms from outside the city and region.

2.20   The 1920s and 1930s saw significant growth in many Birmingham industries e.g. electrical engineering, motor vehicles, cycles, aircraft, other metal industries, foundry processes, iron, food processing, jewellery. The West Midlands and especially Birmingham did not suffer so much from the 1930s depression as many other areas. Birmingham and Coventry had lower than average unemployment rates at the peak of the depression in 1931, but the Black Country, with its dependence on basic metals, suffered badly. After 1931, unemployment in the West Midlands fell rapidly. By 1936, with national unemployment at 13.9 per cent, Birmingham recorded a level of under 5 per cent. The South-East and the West Midlands led the recovery in national employment and output levels after the 1930s depression. Birmingham escaped the worst of this recession. As we shall see, this was not to be the case in the 1980s recession when the local economy had few of the national growth sectors within it.

2.21   Higher wages and available jobs reflected the relative prosperity of Birmingham in the late 1930s and many migrant workers from Ireland, Wales and Scotland, together with many from other parts of England were attracted to the City. Many found accommodation within the Urban Priority Areas of the 1930s. The national rearmament programme boosted the City economy and expansion of manufacturing and increasing prosperity stimulated suburban building without parallel elsewhere in Britain. There was great confidence in the future. Professional, banking and other services expanded to meet the needs of higher manufacturing activity and the growth in per capita incomes. The 1930s also saw increased local authority activity in urban renewal and slum clearance. Families from the Urban Priority Areas were moved to new council estates on the edges of the City. During the 1930s some 8,000 slum dwellings were demolished, but much remained to be done. Many Urban Priority Area residents benefitted from improved housing away from the inner city in a better environment of low density estates consisting of terraced and semi-detached housing, with gardens of their own.

The Second World War and its Aftermath

2.22   The 1939 war provided a significant boost to the Birmingham economy and opened up employment to women on a much larger scale than hitherto. After the war industrial and regional policies of the government constrained the growth of Birmingham. By 1951 nearly three-quarters of Birmingham's manufacturing labour force were employed in motor vehicles, engineering and metal goods. The City of one thousand trades had become heavily reliant on a few growth industries of the 1930s. In the 1950s through to the mid 1960s the West Midlands and Birmingham workforce enjoyed relatively high wage levels as economic activity accelerated. The foundation was a seemingly strong specialized manufacturing base. Industry was larger scale, less diverse, and locally interdependent. By 1973 the West Midlands County area (West Midlands conurbation plus Coventry) had a lower proportion of small firms than the national average and a high proportion of firms employing over 1,000 people. Thus the employed population of Birmingham relied to an above average extent upon large firms. This development meant increasingly that decisions about Birmingham industries (especially the larger ones) were less likely to be made in Birmingham, but rather in London or overseas.

2.23   Government national economic planning policy encouraged industry to move to the less prosperous areas of the country.
Firms wanting to extend were encouraged to locate factories outside the conurbation. This policy and the need to have an Industrial Development Certificate to expand in Birmingham constrained and discouraged increased investment within the region, at the same time diverting any new industry away from Birmingham and the West Midlands conurbation. Thus natural industrial self-generation was hindered. For an economy based heavily on manufacturing this was important.

2.24   The growing congestion of factories and workshops often intermingled with dwellings in the older Urban Priority Areas, and industrial dispersal policy, encouraged firms to leave. But the evidence is that firms often did not move, but rather stagnated or ceased to exist. The old core industrial area of Birmingham lost 42 per cent of its factories between 1956 and 1966, 17 per cent moved out of the inner area but 25 per cent went out of existence. Only 17 firms moved into the inner area while 262 moved out; some 160 firms had started there, while some 515 had ceased to exist in any form. The cumulative impact upon the employment prospects of Urban Priority Area residents in particular was severe.

2.25   Birmingham and Coventry were second and third only to London in the growth of new jobs between 1951 and 1961. The late 1930s home market economy was transformed in the 1950s to an export market led demand for electrical engineering and motor vehicles. Even after the initial advantage of low levels of foreign competition had been lost, the West Midlands industries, contributing up to 40 per cent by value of UK exports, were well placed to take advantage of the expansion of international trade.

2.26   Birmingham's reliance on a few manufacturing industries with their key trades unions was challenged in the 1970s and 1980s by increasing competition from overseas, especially in the motor car industry. At the same time growth in the service and distribution industries was slow and by no means compensated for jobs lost in manufacturing. New service sector jobs were often female, part-time and generally low paid. Those jobs being lost were often male, highly paid, skilled jobs.

2.27   By the 1970s Birmingham's prosperity substantially depended on interconnected industries which were vulnerable to competitive challenge in both home and export markets. The motor cycle industry is one example of industries which had grown and were able to flourish in a protected environment. But from the mid 1960s, the reduction in tariffs on industrial goods, the reduction and eventual elimination of Commonwealth preferences, exposure to free trade with entry to the EEC and changes in production processes (especially the technological revolution in motor vehicle manufacture) and changed transport costs opened up imports from newly industrializing countries.

2.28   Economic growth in prosperous times was patchy. Some firms moved out, others did not survive. Birmingham lost both people and jobs to other areas. In the 1970s and 1980s towns like Stratford-on-Avon, Warwick and Leamington prospered relative to Birmingham. Birmingham's industries needing to compete in home and export markets were often compelled to move or expand out of the City. A vigorous campaign by the West Midlands County Council before abolition in 1986 and by Birmingham City Council concentrated on developing new industrial sites in the city.

Housing

2.29   We have already seen that housing improvements were minimal through City Council action in the late nineteenth century. Bye-law standards relating to dwelling construction, residential space and street widths gradually improved the quality of housing areas. After 1919, national legislation enabled the City to build dwellings for the working classes and after a slow start Birmingham became a vigorous council house builder. However, until the 1935 slum clearance programmes, policies were largely aimed at those families with sufficient income to afford council rents. The poor were left behind. The most significant feature of Birmingham in the inter-war years was the building of large numbers of new homes on the City fringes in large estates e.g. Billesley, Kingstanding.

2.30   The slum clearance programme of 1935 was the first real attempt to replace old, unfit, unhealthy housing, with new council estates away from the city centre. There was useful voluntary work which helped to improve the living conditions in Birmingham's slums, but its total impact was small. Before the building of council houses on a large scale in the 1930s, Urban Priority Areas were associated with the inner, older, housing areas of the City. In effect the advent of council housing often resulted in redistributing Urban Priority Areas, though newer estates would not have been recognized as such as in the 1930s.

2.31   Housing pressures in the City remained immense. In 1914 19 per cent of houses were occupied by 2 families or more, by 1922 this had become 30 per cent. The City built over 50,000 municipal houses to house over 200,000 people between 1919 and 1939 (13,000 of them by 1922). During the same period 54,500 private houses were built. A consequence was the rapid growth of suburbs, often housing people on low incomes.

2.32   Despite all this activity the scale of the problem remained immense. In 1935 there were still 38,773 back-to-back houses, 51,794 houses without a separate W.C. and 13,650 without a separate water supply. The position was much more serious than in many other cities. By that time the City Council had accepted the need for its housing policy to assist the poorest families in the City in a more comprehensive manner than before. By 1939 the council had begun to consider more directly the amenity needs of the new estates — which were essentially areas of pleasant low density housing but with few facilities. But the Second World War intervened.

2.33   The Second World War resulted in a serious deterioration in Birmingham's housing stock. 5,000 dwellings were destroyed by bombs and by 1945 some 100,000 people lived in totally inadequate housing dating from before 1870. The problem was not simply structural, for there were high levels of overcrowding and housing densities were excessive. The poorly built slum dwellings were intermingled with factories, workshops and warehouses, typical of nineteenth century development. The major housing problems and the worst Urban Priority Areas were near the City centre. After the war some 51,000 unfit dwellings were identified and the council compulsorily purchased property in five central redevelopment areas and rehoused 100,000 people in 30,000 houses. There was also a huge waiting list for council houses and only one quarter of all new houses were planned for slum clearance. This was totally inadequate and the position was made worse by the initial inability of the City Council to develop its building programme as speedily as other cities.

2.34   By the early 1950s the rate of slum clearance and rehousing was at the rate of 1,000 families a year, but high rents and suburban living costs deterred many slum dwellers from accepting council accommodation. By 1952 the process of central redevelopment area clearance and renewal had begun, but only half the residents displaced could be rehoused in the same area. There was, as a result, massive displacement of population to the periphery and, later, to new towns. By 1963 Birmingham had overcome these early deficiencies and housing renewal gathered pace so that by 1966 Birmingham was renewing itself faster than any other city in Europe. The central area redevelopment was almost over by 1970 — the landscape had been dramatically changed on a scale unparalleled in Britain. Much of this redevelopment in the centre and development on the periphery of the City made use of new industrialized building techniques for the construction of high rise blocks of flats. By the late 1980s many of the blocks have developed serious structural problems.

2.35   Thus the solutions to the post-war housing and slum problems of 1945 were in some ways a false solution to a perceived problem. Often the more fundamental social problems of communities had not been tackled. Polarization of different kinds of residential communities reflected major social and economic differences between the 'haves' and the 'have nots' of our society. The break-up of communities, the lack of security and the splitting of kinship groups created many problems. A looming problem for the 1990s is that Birmingham has the largest number of tower blocks of flats of any municipal authority in Europe.

2.36   Meanwhile, in the middle ring areas where houses have been renovated, immigrant unskilled workers have tended to settle. Two factors have influenced this. Many could not afford to buy, at least initially, and did not qualify for council housing because of the requirement of previous residential presence in the City. Thus successive groups of Welsh, Scots and Irish, followed in the 1950s and 1960s by West Indians, Indians, Pakistanis, East African Asians, Vietnamese and others, have settled in the middle ring housing areas such as Sparkhill and Handsworth where many old properties face environmental and housing defect problems. We return to this in Chapter 5.

2.37   The City's housing stock is deteriorating at a faster rate than the public and private sector can renew. The City has major housing problems if all its residents are to be housed in decent, modern and acceptable conditions. There has been significant housing development in the 1960s and 1970s which has done much to improve the physical housing conditions of the City, but unfortunately it has not been sustained in the 1980s.

Immigration

2.38   The constant inflow of migrants is a major feature of urban life. People are attracted to the City in order to find work, to improve their quality of life, and to participate in the expected opportunities presented by urban industrial growth. Nineteenth century Birmingham expanded its population by drawing migrants from a wide area of the UK. Some migration patterns have been maintained over a long period, in particular from Ireland and from Central Wales. The most dominant pattern of migration in the early years of growth was that of short distance migration to Birmingham from the rest of the West Midlands. Many workers from other parts of the West Midlands had acquired relevant skills already, others were trained by local firms. At the same time there was a heavy demand for semi-skilled and manual workers in sustaining and developing the economic base of the City. Many of these migrants initially lived in bad housing conditions.

2.39   After 1945 there was significant growth in the demand for labour in the City which stimulated large scale migration from Ireland, the West Indies, India, Pakistan and Bangladesh. The scale of this post-war migration can be assessed from the following statistics, which indicate the reduction in the proportions of those born in Britain. In 1951 there were 51,500 residents born overseas; of whom 0.9 per cent were from the West Indies, 6.3 per cent from India and Pakistan and 69.4 per cent from Ireland. By 1961 the total was 100,000 of whom 18 per cent were from the West Indies, 10 per cent from India and Pakistan and 58 per cent from Ireland. The 1950s saw a large scale immigration of workers from the West Indies. The dominance of Irish immigration was declining. By 1982 it was estimated that there were about 90,000 people of wholly Asian origin in the City and about 55,000 of wholly Afro-Caribbean origin, together making up nearly 15 per cent of the total population. About two-thirds of these immigrants lived in Soho, Small Heath, Handsworth, Sparkbrook, Sparkhill, Aston, Sandwell and Nechells.

2.40   Cultural differences, reinforced in some cases by linguistic and religious differences have changed the character of large areas.

Many ethnic minority groups live in areas of high unemployment, inadequate housing and poor environmental facilities — in short, in Urban Priority Areas which suffer from multiple deprivation. Those of a similar ethnic origin tend to concentrate in their own communities, often from localized areas of the Indian sub-continent.

The 1980s

2.41   Between 1961 and 1981 Birmingham lost some 15 per cent of its population, mainly from inner areas. Between 1971 and 1981 the older, inner city residential core (the Birmingham Inner City Partnership Core area) lost 17.6 per cent of its population, leaving a population of 272,000 by 1981. Much of that loss has been through planned relocation to new towns (Redditch in particular) and to peripheral council housing estates.

2.42   By 1981 43 per cent of the population in this older, inner city area of 272,000 residents were in households where the head was born in the New Commonwealth or Pakistan (15.2 per cent for Birmingham and 4.5 per cent for Great Britain). Ethnic minority groups were and remain especially concentrated in Birmingham and in its inner residential areas. They continue to grow as a proportion of the population of those areas. These are areas of high unemployment. The unemployment rate in the Birmingham's inner city area was 33.5 per cent in mid 1986 (21.1 per cent in Birmingham and 11.9 per cent in UK). By early 1988 the City level of unemployment had fallen to 11 per cent, but the Urban Priority Areas retained relatively high levels of unemployment — over 20 per cent in central wards and much higher in smaller localized neighbourhoods.

2.43   After the 1960s unemployment rose significantly in Birmingham and the West Midlands. By 1983 the regional umemployment rate was 23 per cent above that for Great Britain as a whole. Job losses were particularly severe in vehicle and metal manufacture (where between 1971 and 1981 some 40 per cent of jobs were lost) and in the metal goods manufacture and mechanical engineering industries. In particular job losses occurred in 1971–72, 1975–76 and 1978–81. Between 1971–1983, within the inner city area, there was a 46 per cent decrease in manufacturing employment and a 41 per cent decrease in construction industry employment, the latter striking specifically at inner city residents as the reduction for Birmingham as a whole was only 3 per cent. Inner city residents have suffered to a disproportionate degree from the effects of umemployment, especially long-term unemployment.

2.44   High rates of unemployment are experienced by the young, the over 50s and those living on the peripheral council housing estates. In this respect the young in the inner city, especially if Asian or Afro-Caribbean, are suffering most of all. As employment increases the relative disadvantage of these groups is magnified.

2.45   Since 1986 the general trading position has much improved. Productivity per worker and total output are higher and growing to levels matching or exceeding those of 1979. Profits are increasing. Amongst other things, exports and the consumer booms of 1986 and 1987 have fuelled growth. The motor vehicle industry is making up lost ground particularly in terms of exports (though only after £2,000 million of direct government funding assistance was provided over 1977/8 to 1983/4 to Austin Rover). Some manufacturing sectors are taking on more labour, but others continue to shed workers. Much of the engineering and vehicle industry has recently improved output and productivity.

2.46   Birmingham was allocated Assisted Area Status in 1984 following the review of regional development policy. In 1988 Regional Assistance Grants were abolished in favour of targetting on particular firms. Birmingham and most other areas in the West Midlands also qualify for EEC Regional Development Fund resources. At the same time Birmingham City Council is actively developing measures to encourage the improvement of its local economies, provide job protection and new job prospects. Inner city resources and associated initiatives are aimed at tackling many of the problems of the inner cities. Voluntary groups are often providing a local impetus to job creation or enhancement of the quality of life of those who are unemployed. Private sector resources are increasingly drawn upon to assist Urban Priority Areas.

2.47 Public, private and voluntary organizations and individuals all have an important part to play in getting Birmingham back on its feet. The National Exhibition Centre, the Convention Centre, and the Olympic Games bid are good examples of such co-operative attempts to create an improved image of Birmingham and encourage job creation in the service sector.

Urban Disparities and Urban Priority Areas

2.48 In conclusion we identify three key factors which explain the present circumstances of Birmingham's Urban Priority Areas.

First, in the nineteenth century with its rapid urbanization and industrialization, urban areas were compact, crowded and congested. In the twentieth century, particularly since 1945, we are witnessing a dispersal of population and industry away from the cities. This dispersal is highly selective. Those who can afford to do so often move out. Such selective dispersal emphasizes existing disparities. The unskilled, the elderly and other similar powerless groups are left behind in the Urban Priority Areas.

2.49 Second, although industrial adjustment has always taken place it is now more fundamental and large scale. New technology means less labour is recruited, while that which is required needs a greater degree of knowledge, training and skill. Much of this job loss comes within 20 years or so of large scale migration from overseas into Birmingham to provide a necessary and sufficient workforce to meet needs very different from those now required.

2.50 Third, disparities in quality of life are not wholly based on place of residence. The clearance of central areas after the mid 1950s and the building of peripheral estates have done much to improve the physical housing conditions of many low income families and individuals. Many have benefitted in this and other ways in the City. Nevertheless many economic and social problems remain. The dispersal of the disadvantaged does not solve their problems, it merely relocates them.

Chapter Three

A HISTORY OF CHRISTIAN CHURCHES IN BIRMINGHAM

The Christian Presence

3.1   This chapter provides a brief history of Christian Churches in Birmingham and the role they have played within the City. When Birmingham expanded and industry grew in the nineteenth century, the City was predominantly Nonconformist in its active Church life. The old dissenting families, with their tradition of religious freedom and independence, became rich and powerful. There was no strong Anglican or Roman Catholic presence.

3.2   These characteristics of the Christian presence in Birmingham (particularly influential in the nineteenth century) derive from the impact of the Five Mile Act of 1665, not repealed until 1811. This banned non-Anglican ministers from preaching or visiting within five miles of any city, town corporate or borough. The Act did not cover developing urban centres like Birmingham which were not incorporated. As Birmingham grew in the eighteenth and nineteenth centuries Nonconformists of strong character and conviction came and trade and wealth tended to be concentrated in their hands.

Expansion and Diversity in the Christian Faith

3.3   Eighteenth century Birmingham saw a growing diversity of Nonconformity. Quakers had an influence often out of proportion to their numbers. They were already meeting informally in Birmingham houses in the 1650s, and by 1702 had built the first of two meeting houses which preceded the present one in Bull

Street. Other local meetings were later started, especially on the south side of the City.

3.4 In 1737 the Birmingham members of the Bromsgrove Baptist Church separated to form a church in Birmingham. John Wesley first preached in Birmingham in 1743 and the first Methodist Chapel was established in Steelhouse Lane, but later transferred to the Old Play House in Moor Street. The Presbyterians had several meeting houses, but their congregations became divided with the influence of Unitarian belief and in 1748 the two groups parted — the Trinitarian section linking with Congregationalists and establishing the first Carrs Lane chapel in the same year. The Unitarians had several prospering congregations in Birmingham in the eighteenth and nineteenth centuries.

3.5 From 1715 the Church of England in Birmingham comprised the parishes of St. Martin and St. Philip. After 1774 four new churches were built. They were St. Mary, St. Paul, St. Bartholomew and Christ Church. As the nineteenth century progressed, new churches, chapels, meeting houses, missions and schools of all denominations were opened as Birmingham expanded. The Roman Catholic Archdiocese of Birmingham established in 1850 preceded the creation of the Church of England See of Birmingham in 1905 with Charles Gore as the first Bishop of the new diocese. He resigned the see of Worcester to become the first Bishop of Birmingham and lead the Church in a new response to city life. A leading scholar and Christian social thinker, his commitment to social issues set the pattern for the Church of England's increasing influence, along with the Roman Catholic Church, on the life of the City in the twentieth century. In the nineteenth century Nonconformist influence on Birmingham's religious, cultural, social and economic life was very significant, though the place of Church of England evangelicals such as Canon J. C. Miller, a Rector of St. Martins, is often underrated. Nonconformist and Unitarian families had increasing power and status. The chapel was not only a religious meeting place but an intellectual, cultural and political centre.

3.6 In the nineteenth century, as discriminating legislation was repealed or fell into disuse, the Roman Catholic presence became stronger in Birmingham and in 1841 the first cathedral to be built in England since the Reformation, Pugin's Saint Chad's, was consecrated. Cardinal Newman played a central role in the re-establishment of the Roman Catholic presence in Birmingham. The Irish immigration of the late 1840s and subsequently, accelerated and consolidated the re-establishment of the Roman Catholic Church in

Birmingham and many central and suburban churches and schools were built.

3.7   Birmingham Nonconformists in the later nineteenth century were prominent in local politics. Politics and religion were not separated but were seen as complementary. The 'civic gospel' pressed for enterprise and wider responsibility on the part of local government though not in any organized sense. This movement was initiated by some of the great ministers of the century, such as Dr. R. W. Dale at Carrs lane Congregational Church, Rev. H. W. Crosskey at the (Unitarian) Church of the Messiah, and Rev. G. Dawson at the Church of the Saviour. These and others insisted that church life, civic life, industrial, economic and social life were all interlinked Christian concerns. The development of local government in Birmingham was influenced considerably by this 'civic gospel'. Many key political figures locally and those representing Birmingham nationally, were strongly influenced by the concerns of these Nonconformist churches.

3.8   Richard and George Cadbury, who were prominent Quakers, moved their chocolate business from Bull Street to Bournville in 1879. The new factory provided pleasant working conditions and sports facilities; the surrounding area was developed as a model garden suburb. Leading Quakers played important roles in the life of the City and nation. Joseph Sturge used the power of petitions and public protest on moral political issues. Known nationally for his campaigning against the slave trade, he was an advocate for the advancement of working people and adult education. The Adult School movement arose from Quaker initiatives. John Bright was a Liberal Member of Parliament at a time when Birmingham was a centre of Radicalism. As well as Cadbury, the Albright, Barrow, Gibbins, Lloyd, Southall and Tangye families were examples of influential and prosperous Nonconformist industrialists. Many of them served on the City Council. Unitarians particularly played an important part in city life and had significant roles in local government and in pioneering many civic schemes. Among them were members of the Beale, Crosskey, Kenrick, Lee, Martineau and Nettlefold families.

3.9   There are many examples of Christian social initiatives. Father George Hudson, ordained priest in 1898, developed a complete system of homes for needy Catholic children, who until then had been cared for mainly in Poor Law Institutions, or were simply waifs and strays. The Salvation Army, founded by William Booth with the aim of reaching out to the poor in the large cities, played an important role in welfare provision in Birmingham, providing hostels for the homeless, youth work, work with the elderly and outreach work in local communities. Congregationalists were active in the nineteenth century in the provision of child welfare, food, clothing clubs, excursions, holidays, libraries and youth organizations. Birmingham Nonconformists agitated in favour of government controls over child labour, housing and sanitation. Special chapels were erected in Birmingham for boatmen on the canals and for those constructing the nineteenth century railways and roads.

Change and Reappraisal

3.10   In the twentieth century the Churches found that the Victorian legacy of church buildings became increasingly mismatched with the population. The Church of England reflected the general pattern. Between the two World Wars nineteen churches were built, fifteen of which were in the newer suburbs. The number of churches in the central area reduced because maintenance costs of redundant buildings drained resources which could be more usefully deployed elsewhere.

3.11   Depopulation of central Birmingham began to affect many congregations by as early as the 1870s. In 1897 Christ Church and St. Peter's were closed. St. Mary's and St. Bartholemew's were closed between the Wars; St. Thomas' in Bath Row was destroyed by bombing, and eight other churches were abandoned between 1945 and 1955, either because of damage or as part of large-scale slum clearance schemes. In 1956 Bishop Wilson launched a public appeal, 'Circles without Centres', for £1.2 million. Churches, industry and the Church Commissioners responded so that new churches were built at such places as Shard End, Rubery, and Quinton.

3.12   There is now pressure for change and reappraisal of the role of churches in the inner city areas, particularly in the context of large scale immigration into these areas from the West Indies and the Asian sub-continent. Many of the latter are adherents of other faiths, especially Islam, Hinduism and Sikhism. In the inner city Urban Priority Areas people of other faiths now outnumber those of the Christian faith.

3.13   In many instances congregations in the old churches and chapels tend to be small and eclectic, sometimes leading to partial closure. Many churches and chapels in the inner city struggle hard to prevent decline. Some have forged links with those of other faiths in Urban Priority Areas. For example close association has been established by a local church with the Sikh community in Small Heath. Some chapels and churches have let or sold premises to other faith groups, or to newly emerging Christian groups in the inner city including the Black-led Churches.

3.14   There is now a much greater degree of purposeful co-operation between Christian denominations. This is particularly apparent in new residential housing estates such as Chelmsley Wood and other council estates or redeveloped areas of the inner city. Among local ecumenical projects in Birmingham on the outer estates of Hawksley, Frankley, Chelmsley Wood and elsewhere, Church of England and Methodists share buildings and often worship and witness and have established Anglican/Methodist schools. The Birmingham Council of Christian Churches was formed in 1951 to encourage and promote ecumenical projects and other interchurch co-operation and initiatives. It provides an important means of communication and mutual understanding between Churches in the City and is active in bringing matters of common Christian concern to the attention of those with authority and power.

3.15   There are many examples of the way in which churches have adapted to new roles. Carrs Lane Church, now part of the United Reformed Church, with falling numbers, has taken on a wider role in social, cultural and voluntary activity particularly focused upon the needy, thus maintaining its mission and outreach in changed circumstances.

3.16   St. Paul's, in the Jewellery Quarter, was originally a middle-class church in the 1830s, but after the population explosion of the mid-nineteenth century in the central city it changed its role to serve the very different needs of a rapidly growing population of skilled, but poor and largely illiterate, workers. With slum clearance St. Paul's has again adapted to become a centre of specialized ministry relating to industry and the arts.

3.17   St. Basil's has become a centre for young homeless, Trinity Bordesley a centre for homeless men often associated with alcohol abuse. Such changes are a challenge to other churches to consider imaginative alternative uses of buildings when their neighbourhoods undergo major change.

Black-led Churches

3.18   In any review of the life and role of Christian Churches in

Birmingham, especially where particular concern is directed towards the inner city Urban Priority Areas, attention needs to be paid to the life and role of the Black-led Churches. These churches include the United Church of God, Shiloh, Light and Life, Church of God of Prophesy, New Testament Church of God, Apostolic, Wesleyan Holiness. This history must take account of the prevailing religious climate over the last thirty years with special reference to the reception given to fellow Christians arriving in this country and the difficult struggles and experiences of many Black Christians in retaining their faith in a new environment. This history reflects part of the wider social and economic history of black people in Britain.

3.19   In the first half of this century many West Indians migrated to Central America, Canada and the United States, but in 1954 the McCarran Warners Act imposed quotas on blacks from the Caribbean wishing to settle in the USA. Britain became the new popular destination because of labour shortages after the war and the encouragement given to West Indians to leave their homes and settle in Britain.

3.20   Several points need to be stressed from the black immigrant Christian perspective. First, there was no real help given to West Indian newcomers by Christians or anyone else when they arrived in Britain and Birmingham. It should have been obvious that without help the immigrants would have difficulties in becoming adjusted to a society so culturally different to their own.

3.21   Second,the only group of people who really attempted and succeeded in meeting the needs of newcomers in any meaningful way were the Black-led Churches. This has not been adequately acknowledged in the past. The alienation felt by black people from many of the indigenous Christian denominations was strong. Local Christian Churches often failed to address the issue seriously. Some initiatives were taken — Small Heath Baptists had an Afro-Caribbean minister in the 1960s and West Indian and Asian Chaplaincies were set up in the Anglican and Roman Catholic Churches.

3.22   Third, the pressures on West Indian family life in Britain were enormous. One West Indian wrote: 'West Indian family life in Britain is coming apart at the seams. It is cracking up under the severe pressure of coping with life in Britain. It is demoralized by the onslaught on its traditions and its child rearing practices, by teachers, social workers and other statutory agents and even the children themselves.'

3.23   The black Christians' sense of rejection in Britain is a very significant part of their history. This becomes clear when it has been possible for a black Christian to write: 'Arriving with the warmth of the church I had known, I thought the church, *especially the church*, would have taken me in. Perhaps back home it was my local church where everybody knew everybody, I don't know. But here it was just a blank, grey situation, just like the weather.'

3.24   Some Asian Christians had similar experiences. From the following quotations a clear picture emerges. 'It is very sad, white churches want to spend most time talking to Sikhs, Hindus and Muslims. They do not want to talk to us or care for us at all' (Asian minister). 'Jamaican churches, English churches, they do not want to know' (Leader of Asian house group). 'We have many Sikh friends. They are very surprised to find you English are caring more for talking to them, not to us Asian Christians' (Leader of separated Asian fellowship). We know, however, that in some circles Christians from the indigenous churches were actively involved in action on behalf of immigrant groups. For example Bishop Leonard Wilson brought a vigorous and enlightened concern for the welfare of immigrant communities and was involved in successfully campaigning against discrimination in the City's Transport Department in 1955. He also appointed a Chaplain for Overseas People in 1959. Since then the leaders of Anglican, Roman Catholic and Free Churches have often been outspoken about the lack of adequate concern within the City and society over the problems facing new immigrant groups and were instrumental in establishing what is now the Birmingham Community Relations Council.

3.25   This story of rejection, uncomfortable though it may be to the indigenous Christians in Birmingham, reflects the experiences of many Afro-Caribbean and Asian Christians in the City. It is a story of early rejection, one that only individual Christians and the Christian Churches can hope to reverse.

Other Faiths

3.26   The first mosque for Muslim immigrants was opened in 1941 in Speedwell Road, Edgbaston. A little later a second mosque was established in Sparkhill. Since then mosques have opened in various parts of the inner city including the magnificent purpose-built mosque in Balsall Heath and another recently completed in Birchfield. A Birmingham Council of Mosques has been created.

3.27 In early 1967 the need for a Hindu temple became apparent and an old Victorian house at Hall Road was converted into the Shi Geeta Bhawan Mandir. This was followed by the acquisition of an old redundant church in Heathfield Road which now houses the temple.

3.28 By 1970 there were four Sikh temples in Birmingham and in the following few years others were opened in Small Heath, the city centre and Balsall Heath. Thus the inner areas of the City have witnessed a rapid growth in population of other faiths and the opening of a large number of mosques and temples to provide places of worship — some taking over redundant church buildings.

3.29 Birmingham has one of the oldest Jewish communities outside London. In 1780 there was a synagogue in the Froggery (now New Street Station area). In 1809 a large synagogue was dedicated and in 1856 the Singers Hall synagogue in Blucher Street was erected and is still the main Orthodox synagogue. The Birmingham and Midland Board of Deputies of Jewry plays an import role in city life, in terms of social welfare, industrial and commercial, political and educational activities.

3.30 All these other faith groups widely influence and are influenced by Birmingham society and play an active part in city life; The Birmingham Inter-Faiths Council, which includes Buddhists, Christians, Hindus, Jains, Jews, Muslims and Sikhs, was formed in 1975 to enable dialogue between the different faiths.

Handsworth

3.31 In order to place in some perspective what we have already discussed, this section considers the range of pressures in one particular inner city community, Handsworth, and how they have become apparent in that community. In so doing the Commission has drawn on the experience of an Anglican priest in the area, and his particular perspectives.

3.32 In Handsworth in 1960 the churches were buoyant. A Handsworth Fellowship Committee was set up in 1961 to visit and encourage newcomers. In 1962 the Churches prompted the formation of a multi-ethnic group. The Church of England was able to maintain its traditional role. Since then population and cultural change in the area has led to survival becoming a priority. Many mistakes were made through unpreparedness and insularity by the white churches in the period of rapid immigration of black ethnic groups.

3.33   The Churches in Handsworth often carried on as if there were no changes at all. Few black people were elected to church office. Confidence, vision and the will to develop a wider role in the community ebbed. The Churches stopped meeting together and became more inward looking. Methodist churches were merged and closed, one became a Sikh temple. A Hindu temple took over the Presbyterian church, several churches were sold to new Black-led Churches.

3.34   Other Black-led pentecostal churches grew. They had a deep concern for work with young people, and personal salvation. For good reason they tended to have a strong distrust of existing institutions, especially churches. This arose from black people's experience of rejection. It was also associated with different cultural attitudes to marriage, evangelism, alcohol, smoking and secular social life. Indigenous white people were unable to discern the racial injustice felt and experienced by black people.

3.35   Newly arrived black and Asian Christian immigrants had expected a church-going nation and a welcome as equals in the Christian faith. Generally they found neither. Black church members and their pastors take a clear role in community life as co-workers for the Christian gospel, and see Christian work and witness as incomplete without involvement of the mainstream Churches. Black churches have a strong commitment to the community and to the gospel, and regard other differences as secondary. The majority of these churches seek to work together with others at common Christian tasks. The Handsworth and Aston Forum of Churches (see para 4.40) brings these groups together and is trying to find ways of harmonizing relationships and co-ordinating work in response to social problems. This new development in co-operation has grown out of the disturbances in Handsworth and has had the effect of bringing together black-led and indigenous churches.

3.36   Other Christian immigrant groups live in Handsworth. The most recent are Vietnamese Catholics. Around a hundred families are now settled there with their own Chaplaincy,

Pastoral Centre and a Vietnamese priest at St. Francis (see para 4.25). Asian Christians, many from the Punjab, settled in Handsworth. A number have strong links with St. James Anglican Church (see para 4.38).

Outer Estates

3.37   The needs which local churches encounter and attempt to meet in their neighbourhoods vary. Those Urban Priority Areas situated on the middle ring and outer council housing estates (with few Afro-Caribbean or Asian residents) have very different and difficult problems which provide significant challenges to local Christian churches. There tends to be more formal interchurch collaboration in the outer estates, but, or perhaps because of this, few people may be active church members. Nevertheless the churches often help to create a sense of community, provide facilities for various estate groups to meet, and try to be supportive to those whose lives are affected by the deprivations of Urban Priority Area life. Many church schools are located on such estates and various church outreach organizations are active. Often there is an indifference to all religion, whereas in the inner city Urban Priority Areas life is more frequently influenced by a variety of dynamic religious belief.

Christian Education

3.38   Centres for Christian thinking and education are strongly represented in Birmingham. These include the non-denominational Theological Department of Birmingham University; Queen's Theological College with its inter-denominational composition derived from Handsworth Methodist College and the Church of England Queen's College; Oscott College, training Catholic priests in the Midlands; the Birmingham Bible Institute in Edgbaston and the Central Bible Institute. The Selly Oak Colleges have an outstanding international reputation as a place of training for missionaries, teachers, development workers and other Christians from the UK and overseas. Their Centre for the Study of Islam and Muslim Christian Relations has a world wide clientele and, along with the newly established Multi-Faith Resource Unit and the Centre for New Religious Movements, plays an active part in building bridges between different faiths. The Centre for Black and White Partnership has a national role in providing training for pastors of Black-led churches and for others. There are two church colleges of education in the City, Newman and Westhill

Colleges. The role of Church of England and Catholic church schools is an important one. The Churches have supported the introduction of the multi-faith religious education syllabus in Birmingham schools. This has given a national lead in how to approach religious education in a multi-faith society. The Churches are represented on the local education authority and on its Standing Advisory Council for Religious Education — which produced the syllabus.

3.39   A powerful contribution has been made to the lives of many young people through the uniformed organizations of the churches e.g. Boys' Brigade, Girls' Brigade, Scouts, Guides, and through the Birmingham Council for Christian Education and church-based youth agencies including youth clubs. These organizations are still important and provide a considerable input into youth services throughout the City. The Churches serve many more people than those who attend them, though the range of Christian-sponsored activity is now carried forward by a smaller proportion of the City's population. As history has shown, the significance of the Christian faith does not depend upon the size of its membership (see Chapter 6).

PART II

Christian Responses

4. Christian Responses:
a review of action by Birmingham Churches

Chapter Four

CHRISTIAN RESPONSES: A REVIEW OF ACTION BY BIRMINGHAM CHURCHES

Introduction

4.1 'Power to the Powerless: Theology Brought to Life' is the striking title of a recent book by Laurie Green. It is based on his experience at St. Chad's, Erdington, a parish in the community around the Gravelly Hill motorway interchange (Spaghetti Junction), where the people sought to link theology with action by the Church. He writes: 'We've been helped to discover that theology is not an activity undertaken a hundred years ago, by remote clergymen writing dusty old sermons: it's something that can be done today. It's a practical exercise that involves action, like the setting up of an Advice Centre or whatever, and reflection upon that action.'

4.2 Similarly in 1965, Norman Power, then, and still, Vicar of inner city Ladywood, wrote 'The Forgotten People: A Challenge to a Caring Community'. Crucial housing redevelopment was going on to replace intolerrable slums. His warning was against the scattering and destroying of a social fabric of friendly communities which had kept inner city working class neighbourhoods together, supportive, alive and active. Reflecting in 1987, Canon Power sees the need for building family homes as the basis of developing a stronger sense of identity, community and pride. That emphasis is a feature within current further development in Ladywood.

4.3 These authors emphasize the task of the Church to speak and act on behalf of the community in which it is rooted. Our Chapter 6 on Christian perspectives emphasizes that evangelism and worship may be carried on aloof from community involvement but that credibility and authenticity demand that evangelism and worship must go hand in hand with community service and action. The main responsibility for such action in Urban Priority Areas will lie with Christians in those areas. However, responsibility lies with Christians in affluent areas to lend support to such actions and also to mould ideas, opinions and policies towards a united City through the power they may wield.

Keystones of Urban Priority Area Mission

4.4   We now set out a series of basic requirements for developing effective mission in Urban Priority Areas. We have called them 'keystones' because they are common features supporting most projects. We have drawn these observations from parish submissions to the Monitoring Group set up by the Synod of the Birmingham Church of England Diocese to elicit and receive reports about responses in the Diocese, to 'Faith in the City'. These were collated in a report, 'Responding in Faith', widely regarded as a very worthwhile early response to the Archbishop's report.

(a) *A spiritual base and worship*

4.5   A secure and firm spiritual base of Christian life and experience among the church members provides a strong foundation for outreach. It was seen by many as vital that this secure base was maintained and nourished. Work with local communities requires caring for the spiritual as well as material needs. A parish community worker in Aston said: 'I cannot stress too highly the importance of seeing the spiritual dimension in the work we do in our neighbourhood. While it is good to find ways of improving the quality of life for those in the inner city, it is only when spiritual awareness is discovered by hurt and disadvantaged people that real lasting good is effected'. Worship patterns are developed to reflect this dimension and the diversity of people within local neighbourhoods. Attempts to tailor worship to neighbourhoods suggests worship diversity between churches. Several churches, including St. Luke's, Bristol Street, have developed new forms of worship which are seen as more relevant to local communities within Urban Priority Areas. It is vital that community action and service is not an isolated end in itself but that it flows from Christian belief, commitment and worship. One report has stressed: 'We should like to affirm the programme and projects described in which again and again the emphasis is upon making the good news of Jesus known to local people. In the work there can be no division between service and evangelism, between message and lifestyle.'

(b) *A base in sound information*

4.6   Churches need to understand the environments in which they are working. An assessment of the changing economic, social and physical conditions within their communities is an important foundation for sensitive responses which may be marginal in relation to the scale and range of a community's problems, but can reflect gospel-based concern for the suffering. Assessments could follow the pattern of the Parish Audit in 'Faith in the City'. The Birmingham Church of England Diocese has developed its own scheme, called a Parish Assessment, which most parishes have completed. Some churches have established community activities based on local knowledge, some are unsure about ways of establishing such work. There is a strong case for sharing information and experience between churches of all denominations and with other faith groups.

(c) *Funding and staff*

4.7   Churches were not short of ideas for projects in Urban Priority Areas. Yet many felt the need for a firmer financial base. A variety of sources are being approached — local church funds, trusts, Inner City Partnership, Manpower Services Commission, the Church of England's Church Urban Fund, the Methodists' Mission Alongside the Poor, the local authority, industry and commerce, voluntary bodies, housing associations, Birmingham Co-operative Development Agency, etc. Buildings have been extended, adapted and refurbished for community purposes, by a variety of these sources, often in connection with welfare or job creation projects, particularly through the MSC. Volunteer workers for such projects have come from the local church itself and from the wider neighbourhood. Several church projects have employed people, often on a part-time basis, using MSC, inner city and other funding sources. In future, Church Urban Fund support is likely to be used for employing lay workers.

(d) *Structures of support*

4.8   Support for the Churches' action in Urban Priority Areas is being provided by denominational sources across a wide front — e.g. Church Urban Fund and Mission Alongside the Poor. The Baptist Church employ an Urban Missioner with a roving brief. The Handsworth and Aston Forum of Churches have drawn black and white together in support for local plans. The Birmingham Diocesan Council for Social Responsibility provides some 'pump priming' funding for local projects and a network of support for church community workers. A common response to an area's needs by different churches is a strength — e.g. on the Hawkesley estate where Methodists and Anglicans combine in a church centre run in a Church of England Methodist Church School. 'Twinning' arrangements between non-Urban Priority Area and Urban Priority Area churches are also supportive: though it is important to see that support is a reciprocal, two way flow, a point emphasized in Chapter 6.

(e) *Working 'with' — not 'for'*

4.9   Urban evangelism and community service can be vitally linked. Community development was fostered by many churches, with the recognition of caution over the danger of fostering dependency. Most recognized that community development should be concerned with working *with* people and communities, not simply *for* people. This was seen as an integral part of mission. One church stated: 'The primary commitment of mission being local and witnessing to the social as well as the personal needs is very important if people in the Urban Priority Areas, most estranged from the Gospel, are both to see and hear it. Churches which have evangelism and renewal on their agenda have found a local response.'

(f) *Black concerns*

4.10   Various aspects of response to the place of black people in the Church demand determined attention. A number of inner city churches emphasized the need for black ministers. In particular the needs of the Asian community require special attention through the appointment of Asian workers. There is no room for complacency about increasing the place of black Christians in positions of responsibility in mainstream indigenous churches. In several churches black people were in key positions of authority — e.g. St. Paul's Balsall Heath, St. James Aston and St. Luke's Bristol Street. House groups were seen as playing an important integrating role and St. Luke's was able to report, 'Full integration is taking time, but it is happening amongst the young, local church members.'

(g) *Daily work and the Kingdom*

4.11   Many Christians serve communities and individuals in Urban
Priority Areas through their paid work. They occupy positions
as social workers, home helps, district nurses, doctors,
teachers, traders, a cross section of occupations. Through their work
and actions Christian mission must flow. One church has reported:
'Many of our church members are already very active in community life
and in the caring professions and they should be supported, which
means we should not set up complicated, wholly church-run projects,
and thus add to the burden carried by already heavily committed
people. We must therefore work in collaboration with others'.

Examples of Community Service and Action

4.12   We now set out different examples of Christian witness in local
communities, initiated by individual churches, local churches
working together, or forms of joint Christian action on a city-
wide basis. The purpose of these examples is not for others to copy but
rather to demonstrate the wide range of what is possible. They
represent but a small cross-section of what is happening in the City
today. Some examples have a long history, others have been recently
established.

Birmingham Settlement

4.13   The Birmingham Settlement was established in 1899 to assist
disadvantaged people. Its origins owe much to Christian
concern about the poor in Birmingham at the end of the
nineteenth century. The aim of the organization is 'to seek a better life
for and with people who for one reason or another are denied
opportunities to reach their goals unaided'. The Birmingham Settlement currently operates some 18 main projects. The Settlement
remains concerned that, 'While many people are benefitting greatly
from the economic changes . . . over the last ten years, many others,
although a minority, are not. There seems to be a rise in the scale of
problems among the poor and disadvantaged and more ominously a
frustration because of their feeling that no-one seems to care about
them. A new dialogue is needed between the caring agencies and
community organizations, local authorities, central government and
industry and commerce that commits itself to securing economic hope
for people presently beleaguered and lost in a cycle of poverty . . . The

new effort to create an alliance for regeneration needs to be urgently made a priority so that our society is committed to try to give everyone an equal chance to work for its and their own prosperity.'

4.14   The Settlement has become nationally famous for its work on money and debt advice. Current projects cover money problems, housing debtline, money advice centre, money advice training, the Newtown/South Aston Credit Union associated with the Birmingham Credit Union Development Agency. Members contribute to a common fund enabling them to apply for loans at low interest and avoid the need to go to expensive money lenders. Work with the unemployed includes a drop-in job change project and women's job change. There is a youth electronic music project which attracts a number of unemployed young people from the inner city, an after school club in Newtown and a variety of holiday play schemes. A social worker, community workers and an area caretaker (now funded by the City) operate in Newtown, where there are 27 tower blocks. Other projects include a small number of community flats, a crime victims support unit, an urban ecology centre, day centres for the elderly, student placements for training in social and community work, a women's mid-life centre and a future studies centre concerned with Birmingham's future.

4.15   Much of the Birmingham Settlement's activity lies in the central areas of the City, especially in the redeveloped housing estates and flats of Newtown. In meeting the challenge for funding, five Settlement shops have been opened in the outer suburbs to support action within the inner city. The Settlement employs 84 people and over 300 volunteers help each week. Recently it has undertaken work with Afghan refugees and with the Iranian community in Birmingham.

Housing Associations

4.16   Christians and churches have been active in establishing housing associations throughout the City, over many years, in response to perceived local housing needs. Copec is the largest housing association in the West Midlands with nearly 5,000 dwellings. It was established in 1925 at a time when people felt they had to take action about the appalling housing and other social conditions of that time. Its establishment followed a national conference of Christian Churches on Politics, Economics and Citizenship which was held in Birmingham's Methodist Central Hall in 1924 under the chairmanship of William Temple. In 1970 it merged with Birmingham Housing Trust, and in 1976 merged with the Wolverhampton Housing Association. Other associations with Christian origins include Moseley Churches, Adullam, and Birmingham Friendship Housing Associations as well as the Bournville Village Trust. Much of the Birmingham housing association movement is linked in its history and present with Christian and Church response to improve the quality of housing conditions in the inner city, as well as for the elderly and for others in special need. Housing associations are an interesting example of co-operation of Christians and others.

Birmingham Churches Managing Agency

4.17   In September 1986, with support and finance from the Birmingham Church of England Diocesan Board of Finance, and at the initiative of the Churches Industrial Group Birmingham, the Birmingham Churches Managing Agency was established. As a Community Programme Agency, BCMA works under contract to the Manpower Services Commission to initiate, manage and administer Community Programme employment projects aimed at long-term unemployed people. There are over 100 people working on a variety of community projects primarily within the inner city. These include welfare projects, photography, motor mechanics, tourism and handicrafts. The aim is to reduce substantially the risks of a return to unemployment, or failure to find satisfying and secure work at the end of the one year Community Programme work.

4.18   The Churches Industrial Group was also instrumental in founding two training agencies. These are the Workstarter Unit and the Icebreaker Sales School. These well equipped training centres continue to require support and publicity from city centre and other churches. The Churches Industrial Group is concerned to develop confidence in Birmingham as a business city and encourage churches to take the industrial and economic life of the City seriously.

St. Andrew's Church Centre, Chelmsley Wood

4.19   This is a collaborative venture between Methodists and the Church of England in the largest overspill Birmingham council housing estate, control of which was transferred to Solihull District Council in 1974. It is supported by a team ministry — rector, vicar, Methodist minister, youth and community worker. The Church

Centre provides much needed community facilities which are used by a wide variety of local groups, including Citizens' Advice Bureau, counselling centre, play group, literacy and numeracy classes, mother and toddler groups, centre for the unemployed, dancing classes, large youth centre, and a wide range of evening groups. Bishop Wilson Church of England School is nearby.

4.20   In 1987 a significant proportion of the residents of Chelmsley Wood were owner-occupiers, but twenty-five per cent of the workforce was unemployed — mainly residents who were council tenants. About 100 people are employed on schemes run by the Church Centre in collaboration with the Community Programme scheme and the Queensway Trust. Co-operatives have been started in the area with support from the Birmingham Co-operative Development Agency. A newspaper, the Northern Star, was started by the Church, covering a wider community than Chelmsley Wood itself. The aim was to be a local community interest paper, and to improve the image of Chelmsley Wood. The newspaper is now entirely self-financing, appears once a fortnight and employs three full-time staff. It has developed as a strong and viable community newspaper and has helped to change the previously poor image of the area.

South Aston Church Centre

4.21   This church centre combines two former Congregational churches which built and opened new premises in 1973, just a year after the United Reformed Church was formed. The membership chose to remain in an inner city area and build in the heart of a city redevelopment area. The aim was to become a focal point of the neighbourhood and centre for the community. The approach has been the exercise of a servant ministry, bringing together local people and professional agencies to see what can be done jointly, rather than the paternalistic approach of pretending to know best what 'they' need. The result has been considerable co-operation and a network of trust, with a Christian presence in community life and a general neighbourhood acceptance that the Church is a credible institution.

4.22   In 1978 community involvement demanded new resources and a new project was launched, South Aston Neighbourhood Development. Additional money and premises were found and full-time young adult volunteers were deployed in church and community support work. It has also provided an opportunity for students to be trained in church and community work. A Jamaican minister joined the ministry team for a period and a successor is being sought in order to continue and develop ministry within the multi-cultural church and district. The church's focus on care for the elderly, which brought part-time work for three young people, as well as considerable assistance for the elderly themselves, was awarded a two-year DHSS grant with Age Concern's support. A newly recruited black church members was appointed as Development Officer. She is in touch with about 170 elderly people a week through the twice-weekly day centre, a social club and house visits, and has a team of about 20 volunteers. In South Aston all City departments (Education, Housing, Social Services, Recreation and Community Services etc.), local elected councillors, large residents' association (with its play centre and play leaders, urban farm, market garden, area caretaker, community artist, intermediate treatment worker, sports organizer), and sundry community projects work in close co-operation with the Church Centre.

Mission Alongside the Poor

4.23 In 1983 the Methodist Conference established Mission Along-side the Poor to consider ways in which local Methodist churches could face up to the challenges of helping the poor and needy, especially within the urban areas. Unemployment had risen sharply. Many elderly people were facing difficulties in sustaining everyday activities and contending with loneliness and ill health. It was felt that action was needed. Mission Alongside the Poor provides one of the ways in which the Methodist Church cares for the poor.

4.24 Methodists were asked to give £1 per member each year, over a five year period, for work to be undertaken in inner city, multi-racial and deprived areas. Local churches were also asked to identify community needs and seek appropriate ways of meeting them. In Birmingham and its immediate area five projects are funded by Mission Alongside the Poor, at Stirchley, Lozells, Smethwick, Nechells and Lichfield Road. Community workers have been appointed at Nechells and Lichfield Road churches, a community centre co-ordinator and pastoral assistant at Lozells; improvements have been made to premises at St. John's Smethwick for community work together with a 'Beginagen' shop and a community project at St. Andrew's Church, Stirchley.

The Roman Catholic Vietnamese Pastoral Centre

4.25 There are about 3,000 Vietnamese living in Birmingham, mostly in the Handsworth area. Some 600 or 700 of them are Roman Catholics. The parish priest of St. Francis', the Sisters of Mercy and others have offered friendship and practical help with homes, furniture, English language teaching, introductions to the social services and to Catholic schools. About eighty per cent of the families came from fishing villages, most could not write. A Support Group was formed by the parish priest involving the Union of Catholic Mothers, the Catholic Women's League, the Society of St. Vincent de Paul and the Sisters of Mercy. Two churches were used as centres for Sunday Mass for the Vietnamese Catholics. A Benedictine priest with some knowledge of Vietnamese language and culture came from Coventry to minister to the needs of the community.

4.25   Meanwhile in 1979 Fr. Peter Dao Duc Diem, a parish priest from Vietnam, escaped by sea. He eventually came to Birmingham in 1980 and took up residence at St. Francis' with the parish priest. Fr. Peter not only ministers to the Vietnamese Catholics of Birmingham, but travels to London weekly to minister to the 1,000 Vietnamese Catholics in London, centred around Peckham. In addition he regularly visits Vietnamese communities in other cities. More recently other Vietnamese Roman Catholic priests have arrived in Britain or been ordained here. Fr. Michael Ho Huu Nghia joined St. Francis' church in January 1985.

4.26   The widening scope of Fr. Peter's ministry in Handsworth led to the Archdiocese, in 1982, making available a large converted house as a Vietnamese Pastoral Centre. It has acted as an advice centre especially in relation to housing, schools and benefits, a spiritual centre (for children in particular), and a social amenity. It is an important focus for the Vietnamese community in Britain. As the Centre has developed, the emphasis on advice and information has decreased (which usually meant going along with people to schools, social services, DHSS etc.). The Centre is increasingly used for pastoral work and for the spiritual upbringing of Catholic Vietnamese people. Many meetings and social gatherings take place there. Vietnamese families and single people have been helped to find better accommodation, and many of the younger people who speak English are finding it a little easier to obtain work. From a small beginning of friendship and outreach to a new immigrant community, the Pastoral Centre and its Vietnamese priests provide a service to all Vietnamese families in Britain. It has provided an important element of stability for many Vietnamese families in moving to Birmingham and Britain at a time of particularly high unemployment.

The Centre for Black and White Christian Partnership

4.27   Active steps have been taken to build bridges with Christians from the Caribbean, Africa and Asia, many of whom arrived in the 1950s and 1960s. The Centre recognizes 'the Black churches of the land as equal partners in the Christian Mission. Through the Centre an opportunity is provided to communicate on the basis of mutual respect and partnership and to listen without being patronizing to the voice of our Christian neighbour speaking through another culture.' The Centre is based at the Selly Oak Colleges in Birmingham and is the first such centre to be established. It is sponsored jointly by the British Council of Churches, the Selly Oak Colleges and the University of Birmingham, but is dependent for survival upon gifts from individuals and from Christian communities.

4.28   The Centre works in four fields. It provides a series of courses leading to a Certificate in Theology awarded by the University of Birmingham; it seeks to promote mutual understanding amongst churches in inner city areas; it provides an information resource centre; and it has developed international ecumenical links with churches and other organizations overseas. The Centre has three staff and is responsible to an Assembly representative of churches and other organizations across the country. Based in Birmingham, the Centre is a national centre for Black and White Christian Partnership.

Black-led Churches

4.29   In 1973 Pastor Corbett of the Shiloh church in Aston was concerned that no provision existed for the training of young black people for the ministry. As a result he set up the Central Bible Institute and became its first principal. A linked aim was to enable local people involved with the churches to be more effective in meeting the needs of the area through their ministry. Through his involvement in Aston he became concerned about the pressing social and housing needs of the area, especially amongst young people. This concern led to the creation of the United Evangelical Project in 1976. It was established as an outreach organization and also as a means of drawing the growing number of churches in the area together. Eight churches supported the project (predominantly Black-led). The project has charitable status and is run by a group of trustees from local churches. From 1976–1979 the only permanent funding was from the Cadbury Trust. Later inner city funds were allocated to the project and currently it is funded largely by resources from the City Council, through the Recreation and Community Services Department.

4.30   Over time the project has developed to include several full-
time and part-time staff. The services provided includes a
home/schools liaison officer, a mental health worker, two
hostels for accommodating young people who need time away from
their family, and employment schemes funded by the Manpower
Services Commission, as well as a legal advice scheme and a general
advice centre. In many ways the project represented an important
innovation in helping Black-led churches to understand the nature of
government networks within the City. The project helped to develop
links and networks of contacts which could be used by other people.
Pastor Corbett is a member of the Handsworth and Aston Forum of
Churches (see later).

4.31   Other churches have built their own networks and many of the
Black-led churches have used Manpower Services Commission
resources to help fund building extensions and adaptations,
e.g. the New Testament Church of God, and the Church of God
Prophesy.

4.32   The Wesleyan Holiness Church runs a day care centre for the
elderly and has developed craft work with those attending. It
also provides the home of the Pilgrim Social Action Group
which is concerned with three projects. The first is an education welfare
project looking into the history of Black-led churches and their people.
This project is funded by the Manpower Services Commission and
prepares educational materials for use in schools. The second project is
examining social issues affecting Afro-Caribbean people and the third
project is a hostel scheme which is run for homeless persons.

4.33   The African Methodist Episcopal Church runs a project for the
unemployed to make and fit locks to the property of the elderly
to give a greater degree of security. The project is based at the
church in Hockley and is funded by the City Council's Economic
Development Unit.

St. Basil's Centre

4.34   This Centre is an example of Christian concern organized
through the creation of a charitable trust. It is based in
Deritend and has as its purpose the provision of accommodation for young men and women, youth employment and training
schemes, advice and information services. The Centre is concerned
with young people in difficulties, in need or at risk in the inner city. St.

Basil's tries to accept young people regardless of background, behaviour or looks and works with them to gain skills and resources for independent living.

4.35   Over the last 15 years, St. Basil's has developed a range of services for young people aged 16–25. These include the Boot Night Shelter for homeless young men, providing three weeks accommodation; Tennyson House for particularly young and vulnerable homeless men, offering up to a year's accommodation; Yardley House for girls, providing accommodation for up to three months; Trentham House for mothers and babies, providing accommodation for up to a year; and hostels dispersed around the City which accommodate about 50 young people for up to a year. The Kiosk offers information and advice to 12,000 young people a year, and the Link, which is a housing aid and referral centre, deals with some 1,000 cases a year. Funding for all these projects comes from various sources but mainly Inner City Partnership through Housing and Social Services. A training project assists young black women from the inner city who wish to work in the caring services. Funding is from the City Economic Development Unit. In the first programme, 7 out of 10 women obtained jobs in the field for which they were trained. The whole of the work of St. Basil's is based on the philosophy that creative and constructive assistance to a young person may well lead to a richer and fuller life within the community and society generally. Many of the St. Basil's workers, and others throughout the City, are in the business of helping young people to put down their own roots. One worrying trend at St. Basil's is the falling age at which young people are becoming homeless; for young men it is 15–18 years, for young women 14–17 years. St. Basil's tries to assist at a crucial time of life for many young people.

Birmingham Baptist Inner City Project

4.36   This Baptist Church project was created in 1984 and developed in January 1987 with the appointment of an inner city project worker — an Urban Missioner. The project is located in the Birmingham City Council's inner city priority ring and includes Baptist churches in Handsworth, Aston, Newtown, Saltley, Small Heath, Highgate, Bordesley Green, Balsall Heath and Ladywood. The aims are fourfold. First, the strengthening and encouragement of existing inner city congregations, to alleviate their sense of isolation, weakness and marginalization from wealthier, suburban congregations. Second, to develop mission within and appropriate to inner city needs. This development incorporates worship and spiritual growth, evangelism and practical expression of the gospel in community projects. Third, to take practical steps to understand and relate to people of other faiths and cultures. Fourth, to be a place of theological education and exploration — a resource centre for the wider denomination to pursue further understanding of inner city mission and ministry. The role of the Urban Missioner is to co-ordinate and support the work of the twelve inner city Baptist churches. A report about the Baptist church in Birmingham's inner city is in preparation as is an evaluation of needs and possibilities for help.

Balsall Heath Church Centre

4.37   This Centre is a large multi-purpose building in the inner city
           and is the home of two churches, St. Paul's Church of
           England, and Balsall Heath United Reformed Church. They
sponsor a variety of social and community work based at the Centre;
day care for the elderly with cooked meals served to up to 50 people per
day; a visiting service for the elderly, caring for 600 people in their own
homes; youth work with evening activities, and all-day holiday play
schemes. Many community groups also use the premises. A staff of
some 20 people maintain the work of the Centre, some paid by other
organizations, some volunteers. Funding is from many sources
including Birmingham Social Services Department, Birmingham
Recreation and Community Services Department, charitable trusts,
Church bodies, local fund raising, voluntary donations and rents from
use of the premises. The Centre was dedicated in 1980 and its facilities
are used by the immediate community as well as by other groups where
a base in an inner city, multi-cultural area is relevant. The Centre has
been involved in the campaign to reflect the new image of the area —
the 'Balsall Heath is Beautiful' campaign, which has had important
repercussions in pulling together a strong sense of community
identity,and also in challenging many of the myths about the area itself
— many springing from the days before redevelopment.

St. James Parish Church, Aston

4.38   This and the next two examples are interlinked. This church
           lies in an area of black and Asian majority population, where
           there are enormous difficulties with both overcrowded housing
and high unemployment. The congregation is mixed black and white
with significant black and white working class leadership. A major
Advice Centre has been sponsored, led by a Bangladeshi-born Muslim

organizer. The church finds it has to develop its own workers as no course in social work yet exists in Britain to welcome students who cannot work in English as their first language. The advice centre is active. Over 6,000 separate enquiries were made at the centre in 1985/86, almost double the number in 1980/81. The principal causes of concern were to do with Supplementary Benefit and Family Income Supplement (nearly one-third of all enquiries), National Insurance, passport/nationality issues, housing, gas and electricity, immigration. A small pre-school play group is organized and run by Afro-Caribbean and Bangladeshi leaders working together. A West Indian church neighbourhood worker is funded through the Inner City Partnership. There is a developing working partnership with Roman Catholic, Pentecostal and other evangelical Black-led churches. Through this church partnership — the Handsworth and Aston Forum of Churches — several new ventures are being established, some of which are referred to below.

4.39 The buildings are shared with two other congregations, the pre-school group and the advice centre. Other Aston centres or groups with which the church is associated include: the Residents Association; area caretaker; a language project, initially a church sponsored group, working with Bangladeshi and Pakistani young people and women; the North Aston Community Association linking Afro-Caribbean, White and Asian groups; the West Indian chaplaincy of the Roman Catholic Church; The United Evangelical Project, a Black-run project emanating from the Black-led churches (where a Legal Advice is based); the South Aston Community Project, sponsored by, but separate from the United Reformed Church, running an adventure playground and related youth work. Integration within the multi-ethnic community and between the various Christian church groups is an important aspect of this work at St. James.

Handsworth and Aston Forum of Churches

4.40 Following the disturbances in the City in autumn 1985 this inter-church group was established. It is currently working on the development or extension of four projects. These are, first, the development of a legal advice scheme to ensure that local people have access to proper legal support as necessary. Second, the development of a church-based Credit Union. Many banks in the area have closed and money lenders at high interest rates are active; the Credit Union is attempting to overcome a severe problem for many. Third, employment schemes to create worthwhile work in the area for local people are under way and others are planned. Fourth, the expansion of youth work. The Forum also has ongoing links with the local police. The training and employment schemes include training for local people in business studies, computing, marketing, secretarial services and accounting. Four community care teams have been created to assist and help the elderly and housebound. A team of 10 people are running 'Handsworth Connections', a local community magazine. The Olive Branch Community Care Scheme employs people to work with under-fives, with the elderly and in youth work. The Forum has strong and interconnected links with Handsworth Breakthrough and is trying to develop a wider strategy and wider involvement in churches.

Handsworth Breakthrough

4.41   Handsworth Breakthrough was created in 1984 just before the
September 1985 Lozells disturbances (often inaccurately referred to as the Handsworth riots). It arose to show how the
churches can come together in an area and can be used to meet the
needs of the community. Handsworth Breakthrough began by developing a greater understanding of the area and its communities. Many
Afro-Caribbean and Asian young people have a strong attachment to
the area.

4.42   In Handsworth in 1986 there were 58 church congregations,
compared with 38 in 1960. Thus growth in the number of
church congregations has been high. The congregations vary in
size from 30 to 400, but over 20 have congregations of over 100. The
Handsworth churches have contributed to housing provision, under-
fives provision and playgroups, playschemes, youthwork, advice
centres, education, provision for the elderly, and mental health care.
There are now meetings on a regular basis, of local ministers and
leaders. Regular contact with local authority services and others is
maintained. Handsworth Breakthrough has helped to create a network
of links within its area in order to improve the prospects of influencing
events. With other bodies, such as the Handsworth and Aston Forum
of Churches and the Summerfield Foundation, it has succeeded in a
way which would not have been thought possible three or four years
ago. The Summerfield Foundation is an umbrella community organization, funded mainly by the City Economic Development Unit,
Handsworth Task Force and various charitable trusts. It supports other
voluntary groups and is developing a credit union for cheaper loans and
several co-operative and local employment schemes.

Greenspring, Winson Green

4.43 This scheme operates from units 5 and 6 on the Benson Industrial Estate, Hockley. It is a Community Training Resource sponsored by the Bishop Latimer Church, Winson Green, and supported by Birmingham City's Economic Development Unit and the Manpower Services Commission (two year YTS programme). It trains people in skills concerned with building, engineering, administration and office skills, computer and information technology, furniture, timber and allied trades. Greenspring's philosophy is that 'training is a first and vital step towards unleashing the potential of people to contribute to the society in which they live. Greenspring believes that local people are able to effectively run their own organization . . . Greenspring focuses on people as individuals, using their skills and resources to enable them to contribute positively in the collective society of the inner city.' It also aims to enable people to take the first steps towards combating disadvantage and discrimination, and to enhance the level of economic activity in Rotten Park and Winson Green.

City-Wide Action

4.44 Many churches are engaged in active campaigning on behalf of groups of people both at the City level and nationally. The Christian Churches have a strong tradition in this area of campaigning on behalf of the disadvantaged. In particular the Salvation Army has played a significant role, especially in providing accommodation for the single homeless and in welfare work. The Quakers, along with other Christian Churches and interdenominational bodies, have demonstrated concern and acted on issues of social policy. Whilst small in numbers Quakers are campaigning and taking action in several areas of concern in Urban Priority Areas — welfare work at Winson Green Prison, peace education, housing and poverty. They have shown concern over the use of plastic bullets and the nature of policing in Britain and have been in touch with the Chief Constable and Police Consultative Committees. The Birmingham Council of Christian Churches works with voluntary agencies and with the City Council. It comments to the City Council on issues of concern such as the inner city partnership programme, policies on play, equal opportunities, youth work and multi-cultural education. It works closely with the Community Liaison Section of the West Midlands Police.

Lessons

4.45   This chapter indicates what one group of churches described as 'the willingness of individuals, sometimes in relatively isolated circumstances, sometimes in team or group situations, to tackle difficult and often unrewarding problems, to invest heavily in human ingenuity and human kindness and from the reserves of goodwill and good sense to create genuine "pockets" of hope within the community'. We also need to recognize that many of those of other faiths the inner city are active in community involvement and service. Christians are a minority in many inner city areas.

4.46   There are difficulties with community service and action, particularly related to lack of stability in funding especially the problem of time-expired short-term funding. Community work must develop strong roots in the life of the community it serves, otherwise churches' efforts may become simply superficial. There is a need to scrutinize the purpose and process of community involvement to ensure action is not paternalistic.

4.47   Given current resourcing patterns, the needs of outer area Urban Priority Areas can easily be neglected. The problems of such areas are often different but their needs can be just as great as in the inner city. In both inner and outer areas we have found Christian hope and active Christian spiritual life and believe that there is much to learn from the present witness of Christians living within the Urban Priority Areas.

PART III

Urban Priority Areas in Birmingham

5. Urban Priority Areas in Birmingham

(a) Introduction
(b) Poverty and unemployment
(c) Economic regeneration
(d) Housing and homelessness
(e) Education
(f) Social care
(g) Recreation and leisure
(h) Order and law
(i) Health and medical care
(j) Inner City Partnership Programme
(k) Conclusions

Chapter Five

URBAN PRIORITY AREAS IN BIRMINGHAM

(a) Introduction

5.1   This chapter outlines the nature of the problems in Birmingham's Urban Priority Areas and some of the actions being taken to ameliorate them. We present our findings under a series of policy headings. Many of these policies interact and are often not to be dealt with by a single agency alone — joint working between agencies is required. Present trends in government policy are reducing the direct responsibilities of local government in delivering services. But we believe that its role as the only City-wide elected body which can speak for all City residents continues to be vital, particularly as an advocate, encourager and co-ordinator of private, voluntary, local and other agencies.

(b) Poverty and Unemployment

Income maintenance

5.2   Nearly one-third of households in the City of Birmingham live at or close to the basic level of Supplementary Benefit (around 340,000 people). There are 170,000 people receiving Supplementary Benefit. Of these 43 per cent are unemployed, 27 per cent are pensioners and the remaining 30 per cent claim for reasons of sickness, disability, or as one-parent families.

5.3   Those receiving benefits are frequently residents of Urban Priority Areas. High incidences of poverty and wider deprivation are particularly found amongst single-parent families, the elderly, ethnic minority groups, the young, and older workers. Poverty is defined in relative terms and the expanding gap between rich and poor only serves to further marginalize those who are unable to benefit from the changing economic fortunes of the City. The vulnerability and the often low levels of self-confidence of many Urban Priority Area residents means that the quality of service provided is particularly important. The DHSS recognizes the need for better relationships between its offices and residents in Urban Priority Areas.

5.4   The housing benefits system (mainly administered by the City's Housing Department) is crucial to the income of many households. About 75 per cent of council tenants receive such payments, and especially in the inner city and inner ring of older housing a high proportion of private and housing association tenants receive such payments.

Debt

5.5   Household debt is often high in Urban Priority Areas. In such areas the proportion of adults without bank accounts is much higher than the national figure of 35 per cent. When credit is needed, finance companies, mail order firms and other money lenders charging high interest are the only possibilities. The Birmingham Credit Union Development Agency cites a typical loan of £100 over 26 weeks as costing £156. Those who can least afford it are charged the most for credit. The pressures on people of indebtedness led to the foundation in 1971 of the Birmingham Settlement Money Advice Centre which pioneered debt counselling in the City and led to the foundation of many Money Advice Centres throughout the country. Money advice essentially seeks to restructure a debtor's commitments to reflect the current ability to pay and has proved a strong force for the alleviation of distress among people in the Urban Priority Areas, as well as being acceptable to most creditors.

5.6   The Credit Union Development Agency was set up by the City Council with Inner City Partnership funding to help provide cheaper forms of credit to poorer people. A typical loan costs 1 per cent per month on the reducing balance of the loan. The Credit Unions strengthen the growth of community spirit in inner city neighbourhoods as people co-operate together on money matters. The spread of Credit Unions is welcomed in the City as a contribution to the struggle to enable people who otherwise could not do so to obtain low cost credit.

Job Loss

5.7   The number of jobs in the City has been falling steadily since the late 1960s, and in the early 1980s they fell sharply. The

City lost 200,000 jobs between 1971 and 1986, leaving it with 410,000 jobs. Since then there has been a slight increase in jobs, reflecting some recovery in the Birmingham economy in 1987 and 1988. The Birmingham Chamber of Commerce has recently reported that general business confidence has improved, orders are up, productivity increasing, and exports improving. But the beneficial effects of growth are not evenly spread. Those living in the inner city and the outer estates are less likely to benefit early from an upturn in the economy. Inner City Partnership Area unemployment remains about twice the national average. In the inner city core area (see map 1.2 on page 158) the rate is about three times the national average. These differentials have held reasonably steady over the last few years, while the total unemployment rate has fallen from over 21 per cent to 11 per cent, from 1986 to 1988.

Long-term unemployment and job training

5.8   Some 19,000 people in the core area had been unemployed for over 1 year in 1986, and in Ladywood 60 per cent of the unemployed had been out of work for over 1 year. In 1986 some 50 per cent of all Birmingham unemployed people had been so for over 1 year and 22,500 people had been unemployed for over 2 years. People in the inner city are twice as likely to be long-term unemployed as those in the outer parts of the City. High levels of unemployment in the inner city are as much due to the inability of people living there to get those jobs available as to the actual lack of vacancies. This highlights the central role that training measures must play if this imbalance is to be rectified, and the need to target such training around those jobs likely to be available in higher numbers in the inner city such as construction skills. At the same time there is a recognized shortage of many skills. This has been pointed out by the CBI and the Engineering Employers' West Midlands Association: both welcome the YTS two year scheme, and draw attention to the need for engineering and new technology skills. An Education Liaison Service was recently established by the Association to interest 12 and 13 year olds in the engineering industry — the traditional base of the West Midlands industrial economy. Apprenticeship schemes have been greatly reduced in recent years. The private sector itself has an important role to play in training the labour force with relevant skills. Liaison between schools and industry is gradually improving.

Job training schemes

5.9   There is a wide range of national and local schemes concerned with training and employment to reduce the numbers of unemployed and to provide training and experience to help the unemployed into jobs. Throughout 1986/87 the government Restart Initiative attempted to channel the long-term unemployed to the most appropriate way back into the labour market through e.g. Jobclub, training, and specialist advice but these do not, of course, create jobs. The fall in unemployment in 1987 and 1988 results from economic growth some of it stimulated by government action. The expansion of government measures helps people compete with others unemployed for available jobs and thus to benefit from the more buoyant economy. In September 1988 the new adult training programme will be launched.

5.10   Recent falls in the number of school leavers and an improved economy have meant that it is slightly easier for young people to get jobs. Nevertheless most 16 year old school leavers still go through the two year Youth Training Scheme as the main route between school and work. (See 5.54–5.86 on education.) The local authority, voluntary agencies, the private sector, and the churches have promoted a variety of schemes especially within the Community Programme and YTS. A higher proportion of Urban Priority Area residents are on these schemes whether they be school leavers or older workers. The Commission welcomes the new adult training programme, in terms of length and range of training, the assessment of individual needs, the programme of directed and practical training, and the special arrangements for people with disabilities and other special needs. We feel there are two areas of concern. First, the incentive offered in terms of weighted training allowance with a lead over benefit will be insufficient from our experience to encourage enough people to make full use of such a training programme. Second, there is a particular problem for those 16 and 17 year olds who are not subject to care orders, and who are not in full-time education or employment, and who because of their special circumstances, e.g. homelessness, may be in no fit state to take up a position on a new training scheme. Measures which deny benefits to those who do not participate in such schemes may not have the laudable intended effect and may result in lawless behaviour.

5.11   Birmingham City Council has played an active role in this field. Amongst its initiatives is the development locally of the EEC-supported Wage Subsidy Scheme and a variety of training measures. The City Training Strategy launched in 1987 aimed at a greater integration of training with other business and community support programmes, by increasing knowledge of training needs (using MSC and Chamber of Commerce data and local surveys of its own in Urban Priority Areas) and by improving co-ordination between training agencies. This is an inter-agency programme. Priority sectors have been identified as construction, engineering, business, tourism, materials processing and clothing. The Council hopes to improve provision by itself and others to assist the long-term unemployed and disadvantaged groups in the labour market. A multiplicity of business aids and advice is available. A Community Enterprise and Small Business Strategy has also been adopted by the City Council, aimed primarily at supporting ethnic minority businesses. A series of local employment studies have been undertaken at Sparkbrook/Sparkhill, Winson Green, Saltley/Washwood Heath, Nechells, and on outer estates at Castle Vale and Pool Farm/Primrose Hill. The aim is to identify employment opportunity and training needs, and to encourage community-based initiatives. The Chamber of Commerce is active, through its services, in advising established and new firms, and an Asian business adviser has also been appointed. Birmingham Venture assists businesses with advice and practical help and acts as a sponsor for YTS.

Birmingham Heartlands

5.12   The City Council and the Chamber of Commerce have come together to form a company, Birmingham Heartlands, to lead the regeneration of a 2,000 acre site in East Birmingham. This is a major initiative, which hopes to help local people train for the jobs likely to be created and to involve the local community of some 45,000 Urban Priority Area residents, as well as help to regenerate the local economy. It provides a major testing ground to combat inner city unemployment. Community Forum, a grouping of residents and tenants associations, was concerned that there were presently inadequate means of involving local people in the future planning of their own community. It is important that such an initiative should succeed and should involve the local community. As with other major city redevelopment schemes e.g. Convention Centre, an aim should be to ensure that local inner city and other disadvantaged people benefit more than in the past from job opportunities in the construction phase, as well as in the subsequent operational phase. Tarmac's Broughton Road scheme provides a good example of this. Adequate and appropriate local job skills training is essential to the success of such schemes.

Labour market and wages

5.13   Changes in the structure of the regional and City economy have skewed the labour market. This affects employment and pay.

A tiered labour market is emerging. The upper tiers have a more skilled workforce, consisting of reasonably well-paid workers in stable jobs. Pay levels are higher and the difference between these pay levels and those in the lowest tier of jobs has widened. Nationally between 1979 and 1985 the highest-earning 20 per cent of workers saw their incomes rise by 25 per cent. Average earnings rose 15 per cent in the same period. The average income of the lowest 20 per cent of workers fell by 5 per cent over that period.

5.14   This tendency is compounded in Birmingham by the rapid decline of the City and region from a high position in the income earning league of regions (i.e. next to the South-East in the early 1970s), to almost the lowest English region by the mid 1980s. Lower tier jobs have different characteristics. They are low-paid, often part-time jobs (17 per cent of all jobs and 37 per cent of womens' jobs in Birmingham) which have limited access to pensions, sickness benefit and holiday pay. Progress towards equal opportunity for ethnic minorities, women and disabled people is slow. This causes anger and concern amongst many ethnic groups. Security of employment for many in this low-pay group has declined. These are the jobs which many Urban Priority Area residents are likely to fill, including many in the public sector, and in health care. Many are excluded from Employment Protection legislation because they are part-time workers or retain jobs for less than 2 years. The unemployment rates for Afro-Caribbean and Asian people are twice as high as for their white counterparts, while unemployment amongst the Bangladeshi community in Birmingham is three times as high. Unemployment of such groups in the inner city arises from many factors including low skill, race discrimination and language and cultural differences.

Equal opportunities

5.15   A growing number of government, local authority and voluntary sector initiatives as well as some private sector ones are aimed at assisting black and Asian unemployed people, e.g. Black Business in Birmingham, Handsworth Task Force, and Inner City Contracts, but their impact has so far not been great. The socio-economic structure of the inner city and the outer estates is biased towards those unskilled or semi-skilled occupations which are more likely to have suffered employment contraction. Women are predominantly employed in the lowest-paid occupations, and by choice or necessity represent nearly 90 per cent of all part-time workers in the City. There has been a tendency for male full-time jobs to disappear

and for part-time female jobs to increase. Women's pay as a proportion
of that of men in Birmingham is about two-thirds.

5.16   Even with government schemes the apparent discrimination
against black and Asian youngsters has not been alleviated.
Those better qualified are often unable to find suitable
employment. Many Asians who are self-employed in shops or small
businesses often work on the economic margin, relying for any degree
of prosperity on their family and working long hours. There are
sweatshop clothing factories which exploit Asian women, while others
work for low pay at home because of cultural constraints. Nearly one-
third of black and Asian men are in shift work compared with one-fifth
of white men. 1 per cent of white men work night shifts compared with
4 per cent of Afro-Caribbeans and 7 per cent of Asians. Further action is
needed to develop more effective measures against racial discrimination,
and to target training and employment opportunities to disadvantaged
groups.

Social security changes

5.17   Changes to the Social Security system were made in 1986 and
1987. Supplementary Benefit was replaced by Income Support
and the Social Fund came into effect in April 1988. There will
be much work in converting existing cases to the new system.
Confusion and misunderstandings are likely. The DHSS hopes that the
quality of service to the public will improve by 1990.

5.18   Social Fund payments cover people on low incomes who are in
receipt of Income Support or Family Credit. They will take the
form of a loan or grant, depending on the claimant's
circumstances and the reason for the claim. The Social Fund in
particular has been criticized by social workers, the probation service,
churches and various voluntary bodies because the amount of money
available locally is cash-limited within any one year, and because of the
enlarged range of discretion. The new system is likely to lead to many
of the poor on welfare benefits being relatively worse off than before.
The proposed introduction in 1990 of the Community Charge, to
replace local rates, is likely to put greater financial pressure on poor
people who are already vulnerable to increases in gas and electricity
prices.

(c) Economic Regeneration

Background

5.19 The events leading to recent heavy job loss in manufacturing industry have already been set out in Chapter 2. Here our prime concern is with industrial and commercial interests and their attempts to regenerate the economy of Birmingham. Since 1986 there has been a resurgence of industrial output. Inner city firms were often most vulnerable because of age of industrial premises, unsuitability for modern production methods, poor access and lack of room for adjacent expansion. There was no market for outmoded or uneconomically produced goods.

5.20 The industrial landscape has changed dramatically over the last decade. New industrial zones with new factory units have grown and flourished — though often employing fewer people than in the past. Examples include the regeneration of areas in Aston, Nechells, Tyseley and Bromford, and the development of major new business parks such as Woodgate, Aston Science Park, and the former Talbot site in Small Heath. There is also a major redevelopment scheme for the East of the City, run jointly by the Chamber of Commerce and the City Council through the Birmingham Heartlands Company. The regeneration of such industry remains a prime concern for wealth generation. Birmingham possesses many of the skills and attributes of a good manufacturing industrial base. The City will need in future a much broader diversity of skills more appropriate to newer industries, many in the service sector or adaptations of older industries. Service sector development and tourism will have a role to play in expanding jobs, as will construction and retailing, but manufacturing industry remains essential to the future of the Birmingham economy.

Recent growth and future prospects

5.21 Nationally industrial output increased by about 4 per cent in 1987, while vehicle industry output was up by about 17 per cent. The upturn in the motor industry is particularly significant in Birmingham and the West Midlands with spillover to engineering and metal manufacturing, on which the industrial structure remains firmly based. The future depends on the prosperity of major local firms, such as the Rover Group, Lucas, GKN, Cadbury/Schweppes, Glynwed, Delta and IMI, as well as the creation and expansion of new businesses. Companies, especially large international ones, are more mobile than in the past, and are able to take advantage of the differences between tax laws, the labour market and other costs in one country compared with another. Most of the new investments in industrial expansion by companies not already in the West Midlands Region are not located within Birmingham, but in the smaller surrounding towns. The West Midlands Industrial Development Association attempts to stimulate new investment as well as encouraging a greater export orientation in the region. Future trading prospects are subject to trading conditions on the home, European and world scene and are affected by international trade, the relative value of the pound, product competitiveness and the degree of stability in international markets.

Appearance

5.22 Derelict land and vacant industrial property have adversely affected the appearance of the City. The success of the National Exhibition Centre, the new airport terminal building, the Convention Centre, the bid for the 1992 Olympic Games, the Super Prix motor race, have begun to attract international recognition and investment. The image of an old, derelict, industrial city has never been just and is being changed, though more remains to be done.

5.23 The City receives various forms of central government aid to assist its regeneration. These includes Regional Selective Assistance under the Industry Acts which, since late 1984, has automatically opened the door to EEC Regional Development Fund Resources. Regional Assistance is now abolished but aid will continue, targetted on specific firms. An Innovation Team within the Department of Trade and Industry attempted to improve the take-up of schemes to encourage industrial growth in the City. Inner City Partnership funds assist regeneration in the inner city area and the Handsworth Task Force concentrates on economic development in Handsworth. The inter-governmental agency, City Action Team, tries to co-ordinate policy across Whitehall ministries. In December 1987 a Cabinet minister was appointed to take day-to-day responsibility for the co-ordination of inner city action under a Cabinet committee chaired by the Prime Minister. The City Council has been successful in gaining Urban Development Grant funding for some private sector led development schemes, such as a Paradise Circus hotel development which employs local labour. Derelict Land Grant has been used to reclaim land for subsequent use. A Freeport has been developed adjacent to the airport. Finally the City Council together with the

Birmingham Chamber of Commerce have created the East Birmingham Urban Development Agency to be run by the Birmingham Heartlands Company (see 5.12). A great deal is being done to assist in regeneration and some of the schemes, particularly training elements, are being funded by the MSC.

Employers' views

(i) Chamber of Industry and Commerce

5.24   The Birmingham Chamber of Industry and Commerce carries out quarterly economic surveys of its members to assess the future for industrial and commercial projects. Birmingham firms were asked to indicate factors most likely to improve their prospects. Three-quarters of companies indicated the need to reduce interest rates, just over a half mentioned the reduction of local authority rating. Two other issues gained between forty and fifty per cent support — higher productivity and reduction of the tax burden on companies. A group of 30 companies sponsor Birmingham Venture (which is also assisted by Business in the Community). It offers advice and assistance to those thinking of establishing a business and to those already running one who require help for expansion. Managers from sponsoring companies are seconded to Birmingham Venture. In 1987 the Chamber created its own Community Programme managing agency to play a positive and practical part in creating training and employment opportunities in addition to running its own YTS training scheme. The Chamber assists the organization of overseas trade missions with others including the West Midlands Industrial Development Association.

5.25   The Chamber of Commerce helped to establish Black Business in Birmingham to assist those with a sound proposition but with poor access to capital, to finance a new venture, or to expand an existing one. Much banking practice is related to loan security rather than business potential. The head of Black Business is a seconded black vice-president of an American bank whose aim is to assist mainly Asians and Afro-Caribbeans, to develop their own businesses. This is achieved through training programmes, funded by the Department of Employment, giving assistance in preparing financial elements of business plans in order to give a greater chance of securing normal bank lending, and through general advice and assistance. Its basic aim is to assist the planning and operation of black businesses and generally to help stimulate a greater proportion of black-led business. It is a small enthusiastic organization which concentrates on small businesses. Its aim is to unblock barriers to small company growth.

(ii) Confederation of British Industry

5.26   The CBI consider that while not all the City's industrial problems are yet over there is nevertheless an attitude of optimism which has not been apparent for some time. The rationalization and restructuring which many companies have had to undertake has left them more efficient and better able to compete in tough markets.

5.27   Unemployment, though declining, remains a key concern of CBI members, as does the problem of industrial dereliction. The only way many industrialists see of finding long-term effective solutions is by creating a competitive industrial structure which will create the wealth to provide for social needs. They say that only a thriving industrial and commercial base, capturing a larger share of world markets, along with the use of public funds to attract private sector investment, can create the employment opportunities which are necessary. A natural result is seen as the revival of Urban Priority Areas. The CBI has declared inner city regeneration to be one of its key concerns over the next few years.

(iii) The Engineering Employers' West Midlands Association

5.28   In 1979 the Engineering Employers' West Midlands Association had 1,400 companies in membership, employing over 400,000 people. In 1987 there were about 1,000 companies employing some 160,000 people. A 1987 report of the Engineering Employers' West Midlands Association concludes that 'the West Midlands has a lot going for it. It has good communications with the majority of the population of the UK and the channel ports are within a day's lorry drive. The image and profile of the West Midlands has been improved. . . . The area is still the centre for manufacturing'. The Association is concerned with the regeneration of employment but does not 'envisage in the medium term any significant increase in employment within the engineering industry; indeed some forecasts suggest further reductions. We do envisage, however, significant changes within the composition of that number; opportunities for unskilled and semi-skilled grades are likely to reduce but there will be new opportunities for machine operators, those offering flexible skills in traditional crafts, technicians, technologists and graduates'.

5.29   The Association is concerned because young people are not showing interest in the engineering industry, and because of the lack of mathematics and physics teachers in secondary schools. An Education Liaison Service has been created to interest school children, their parents and teachers. Some firms have links for fostering interest, job experience and employment with specific schools: for example the Rover Group and West Midlands Gas have such links with Holte School in Aston. Engineering firms contribute directly to training through YTS and welcome the new two-year scheme. The Association is also concerned about the reasons for lack of participation by ethnic minority young people in employer-led schemes. An enquiry is under way which aims to improve the proportion of ethnic minority young people on employer-led engineering training schemes. (See also 5.79 to 5.84 below.)

(iv) Small beginnings

5.30   One company chairman told us that he felt that Birmingham is experiencing a strong economic recovery, but that the recovery cannot succeed without large numbers of small businesses — shops, workshops, service agencies etc. Yet such enterprises face severe problems in some inner city and other Urban Priority Areas, especially in relation to security and vandalism. He felt that the authorities were not doing enough to ensure protection, or make insurance available at a reasonable price. 'It is quite wrong and counter-productive that insurance for a small shop in Aston should cost much more than one in a Sussex village or be unobtainable.'

The City Council

5.31   The City Council has developed an economic strategy, aimed at assisting the creation of a strong local economy offering employment to all Birmingham residents who wish to work. Much depends on the economy's ability to 'export' goods and services to other countries and other parts of the UK. Manufacturing remains crucial, but is unlikely to produce a massive increase in jobs, as higher productivity and new technology bite. More service industries are being encouraged. Some of the schemes which fall under the strategy include an EEC-supported Wage Subsidy Scheme, Meet the Buyers events, consultancy activities to industry, establishing the East Birmingham Urban Development Agency, extending enterprise workshops, Aston Science Park, Birmingham University Research Institute, CADCAM/ Technology Centre, Community Enterprise and Small Business Strategy including local employment studies of inner and outer Urban Priority Areas, including Castle Vale and Pool Farm/Primrose Hill. The

Council supports the West Midlands Industrial Development Agency in its work of publicizing Birmingham industry and assisting the export drive especially in the USA, Japan and West Germany.

Changes in a local inner city economy — Balsall Heath

5.32 In January 1985 nearly 4,000 people were unemployed in Balsall Heath/North Moseley, an unemployment rate of 35 per cent. This was one of the highest rates in the UK for an area of this size. 56 per cent of 16–18 year olds were unemployed, compared with a City average of 35 per cent. There was a high rate of male unemployment at 41 per cent (26 per cent for the City), while over half the unemployed had been out of work for over one year. Even after various training schemes, the chances of young people finding jobs is poor. Many young people were long-term unemployed. Local community workers speak of the difficulty that unemployed people of over 45 or 50 years of age experience in finding another job. The local unemployment rate for those over 45 years of age was 33 per cent (compared to an inner city average of 22 per cent). Asian men in that age group had particular difficulties.

5.33 The industrial structure of Balsall Health/North Moseley showed that in 1985 606 firms employed 8,419 people. There were few large businesses, only 5 firms employed 100 or more people. Half the businesses employed fewer than 6 people and 96 per cent fewer than 50 people. The remaining 4 per cent of the businesses employed 41 per cent of the workforce. Distribution trades accounted for 36 per cent of all businesses — mainly shops (employing 22 per cent of all employees within the area). The largest group of employees (37 per cent) were in other service occupations, mainly local government and the health service. A low proportion of businesses (only 22 per cent) were in manufacturing. Between 1976–1981 there were significant changes in manufacturing. There was a 32 per cent fall in manufacturing jobs (19 per cent city wide), despite a small increase of 4 manufacturing firms. There was a sharp decrease in the number of people employed within medium-sized businesses with 1,124 fewer jobs available in businesses employing over 50 people. The number of small businesses increased, due in part to new businesses, but also due to the contraction of larger businesses. Overall in 1976–1981 62 businesses closed down with a loss of 1,504 jobs, while 66 new businesses started, or relocated within the area, bringing in 801 jobs.

5.34 The City Council has assisted the area through the Moseley

FIC—F

Road Industrial Improvement Area, New Enterprise Workshops, including those at Bath Walk, and new industrial units at Clifton Street. At the same time the area has benefited from the growth of Asian businesses. Ethnic minority groups comprise about half the residents of the area and Asian business growth has dominated the local scene. This is particularly true of the retail sector, where centres such as Ladypool Road have received a new lease of life and continue to remain significant sources of local employment. Some of the Asian restaurants there have achieved City, regional and nationwide acclaim for their food.

5.35   Three other factors stand out. First, many local residents see the popular poor image of Balsall Heath/North Moseley as a distortion of the truth and adding to decline. Local people feel strongly that the press and media, and at times the local authority, emphasize the area's severe deprivation and problems, rather than the positive aspects of its life. Negative publicity does nothing to restore confidence and attract investment — a view shared by the local community newspaper 'The Heathan'. Residents actively campaigning for a better image founded the 'Balsall Heath is Beautiful' Campaign in 1987. It has had success. Second, house prices in many parts of the area are low. Some houses have remained for sale for a considerable time — though by 1987 there was greater buoyancy in the housing market, especially of improved housing in 'enveloped' areas (see para. 5.42). Third, compared to many parts of the City the area has low incomes and a low spending power. Many cannot therefore maintain or repair their houses adequately. Low spending power results in a weak retail economy and deters further investment. However, the economic upturn of 1986 and especially 1987, is improving this situation. Many people are justly proud of living in this area and would like to see more investment in business and jobs, as well as the environment, much of which has already been considerably improved. The problem is that the image of the area relates to its past, not its present. Images take years to form, and are slow to change. But it is clear the local image of this area has changed in a positive, confident, direction largely due to the actions of the community itself.

Conclusion

5.36   The regeneration of industry and commerce and the creation of new jobs is essential to the City. Most of this clearly depends upon the decisions of business people in positions of power. The task can be assisted by the City Council, by local communities, by the voluntary sector and by individual decisions. In order to reduce disparities, investment needs to be attracted to Urban Priority Areas, and appropriate training provided. Many companies operate successfully in Urban Priority Areas, or employ large numbers of people from the inner city or outer estates.

(d) Housing and Homelessness

Housing conditions

5.37   In recent years the lack of both public and private investment has led to deteriorating housing conditions in Urban Priority Areas. The 1980s have seen a reversal of the steady overall improvement in the public and private housing stock which was achieved in the 1960s and 1970s. Without proper maintenance and new building many people remain trapped in poor accommodation and, because they are impoverished by lack of employment opportunities, lower income households find decent housing increasingly difficult to obtain.

5.38   Lack of investment is leading to a spiral of decline in the older, inner city and middle ring housing stock in particular. Restrictions on local authority housing programmes lead to increasing difficulty in maintaining the local authority housing stock. Housing associations are faced with similar problems of inadequate resources to repair and improve existing property. The scale of the problem in Birmingham is severe. It is the elderly, the poor, the black and Asian groups who are hit hardest, whether they are owner-occupiers or council tenants.

5.39   Good housing is vital to the development of home and family life and the creation of healthy communities, in all senses of the word 'health'. Poor housing adds to other pressures upon Urban Priority Area residents, such as low income, unemployment, greater family stress and breakdown, crime, and poor educational achievement. Despite massive slum clearance and redevelopment programmes in the last 30 years, by 1986 about a quarter of the City's 400,000 dwellings were either unfit for habitation or needed extensive repairs. The rate of dilapidation exceeds that of rehabilitation, repair or replacement.

Housing demand

5.40   There is a housing crisis in Birmingham. The population is falling but there is an *increasing* demand for dwellings. It is estimated that 17,000 extra dwellings are needed in the period 1986–1991. The growth in demand relates particularly to small households and the desire of many young people to set up their own homes. Homelessness has increased substantially, especially amongst young people. Despite the tremendous efforts of the City in dealing with its post-war housing situation there remains a problem of major proportions. By 1987 there were 26,300 households registered on the housing waiting list, over double the number in 1979. Some 24,400 council tenants want to transfer to alternative accommodation, particularly from flats to houses. In 1986 7,970 households approached the City as homeless, a figure nearly three times higher than in 1977.

The council housing stock

5.41   There are massive problems connected with the condition of the City's own council housing stock of about 125,000 dwellings. Many inter-war houses are in need of major repair, and particular problems exist with dwellings (low-rise as well as high-rise) of non-traditional construction. Some four-storey blocks of unpopular flats have been 'top-lopped' to create two-storey dwellings with a pitched roof. Botany Walk in Ladywood is an example of this approach, costing £25,000 a unit. High-rise blocks in Caulder Crescent, Beale, Balfour and Clayton houses, also in Ladywood, have had money spent on the exterior to make them safe, as well as improvements inside. In one case, that of Beale House, the local authority was forced to take action because of a court case brought by tenants. That block was not as bad as certain others; it was fiftieth on the list of high rise blocks for repair. Similar repair works have been carried out to high-rise blocks in Chamberlain Gardens. The costs are very high, being upwards of £12,000 per flat. The cost of renovating the total council stock is estimated at £740 million or £975 million if the costs of demolition and rebuilding (together with the City's legal obligation to buy back or repair defective homes sold to tenants) are added. The priority is to repair the dangerous condition of some high-rise flats. This need diverts resources from making basic improvements to dwelling interiors and to older houses and flats. Birmingham is Europe's second largest local authority landlord and has 426 blocks of high flats.

Private housing

5.42   About one in seven private homes (a total of 34,000) are unfit, another 5,800 lack basic amenities. The City has carried out external 'enveloping' work (exterior improvements only) which the City pioneered to bring homes up to present day standards. The costs are estimated at about £400 million. This includes bringing some 4,000 dwellings in multiple occupation up to a reasonable standard. In some areas clearance is the only option, but alternative accommodation is in short supply. This is particularly a problem in the Saltley area and can reduce the speed of home improvement. There are increasing signs of disrepair and poor facilities in inter-war private housing.

Housing costs

5.43 Wider social and economic factors have an impact on housing policy. High unemployment and low incomes mean that some 75 per cent of council tenants receive assistance in order to pay their rent, as do many private and housing association tenants. Increasingly householders are defaulting on mortgage payments and may find considerable difficulty in financing adequate repair and maintenance.

Housing and race

5.44 Many ethnic minority households are severely disadvantaged in the housing market. The council housing allocation system creates disadvantage to ethnic minorities. They are allocated fewer properties than their numbers on the waiting list would suggest should be the case. The Housing Department is attempting to remedy this. Incidents involving racial harassment have increased amongst council tenants from 5 in 1983 to 27 in 1986. We were told by ethnic minority groups that often choice of housing by black and Asian groups has more to do with where they feel physically 'safe', than with the area where they would choose to live. They often get the poorest housing stock, which needs repair, lacks adequate heating and suffers from damp. Young people of the Afro-Caribbean community are allocated an undue proportion of inadequate housing for single, homeless people. White applicants are 4.5 times more likely than black or Asian applicants to get inner city houses rather than flats allocated to them. A monitoring system is operating to try to eliminate this housing disadvantage. Housing neighbourhood offices, which the Commission welcomes, have deliberately recruited more black and Asian staff. The Housing Department and the Birmingham Community Relations Council are attempting to rectify these situations.

Housing the elderly

5.45 There are special problems facing the growing number of elderly people, especially those over 75 years, many of whom require special housing provision. 'Care in the Community' initiatives mean that more people are leaving institutional establishments and need suitable housing, care and support. Some high rise blocks, such as Salisbury Tower, have been successfully converted to vertical warden secure housing schemes for the elderly. Other low rise schemes have been built, such as Golden Croft in Handsworth.

Social housing expenditure

5.46 Britain spends less of its Gross Domestic Product on housing construction than most other European countries. There have been substantial cut-backs in capital expenditure on housing but massive increases in government support for housing benefit payable to households on low incomes. Housing Investment Programme Allocations by central government to local authorities were reduced from £4,248 million in 1979/80 to £1,225 million in 1987/88 at constant prices. Local authorities are restricted in the amount of money derived from land and dwelling sales which they can 're-use' on new housing investment. As a result Birmingham's new housebuilding programme of 1,258 dwellings in 1979/80 was down to 62 in 1986/87. Housing Associations provide fewer than 1,000 new or improved dwellings a year. Urban renewal programmes have also suffered from cutbacks. The only way to provide more money for day to day spending is to raise rents. Since 1980 some 20,000 council homes have been sold to their tenants, of which 97 per cent are houses. This means that the pool of rented houses has reduced. Some council estates now have a predominance of owner-occupation. More and more, council housing caters for a disproportionate share of the more vulnerable and deprived sections of the community. Council housing is increasingly welfare housing. In 1981 35 per cent of households in the City were council tenants, but 49 per cent of single pensioners living alone were council tenants, as were 66 per cent of single parent families. On present trends the danger is that council housing will house the poorest, most deprived sections of the community in some of the worst housing. The Commission views this as unacceptable.

Improving City Council housing

5.47 Despite all this the City has made progress, including the renewal of private sector housing.

(a) Increased provision for the elderly

A limited new build programme has been continued, high rise flats have been converted: in one block in Newtown extra care facilities for frail elderly people are provided. The schemes are popular. The City manages 4,640 sheltered flats and bungalows for elderly people. It has also installed alarms where there is no resident warden. Some 2,500 dwellings are linked to a 24-hour response unit in the housing department's headquarters.

(b) Improvements to flats and maisonettes

Refurbishment of post-war flats has been successful, especially when converted into houses, e.g. in Lozells, Shard End and Ladywood. The costs are high.

(c) Improving environment and security on council estates

These programmes are aimed at reducing crime and vandalism by improving the level of estate management, by mobile teams of cleaners, by NACRO project presence, and by concierges in multi-storey flats, home security measures, police presence, increased lighting and a more secure living environment. The Wyrley Birch estate in Kingslanding is one example.

(d) Improving the repair service

Outstanding repairs have been increasing dramatically. Quick response teams now operate in 10 areas of the City, and recently extra resources were voted to cut the backlog of outstanding repairs from 65,000 to about 30,000 and to reduce the non-urgent repair waiting time from 41 to 20 weeks. £4 million has been allocated, but taken from planned maintenance. Thus yesterday's repairs are done at the expense of the future. The most common tenant complaints are about the repairs service.

(e) Taking services to people

So far about 30 Neighbourhood Offices have been opened, and there are local management offices in some estates, e.g. Bloomsbury (part of a Priority Estate Project), Ingoldsby Road, and the Wyrley Birch Estate.

Offices are 'one-stop shops' for a variety of council services. Neighbourhood Offices provide a range of council services and provide points of easy access for local people. The Commission supports Neighbourhood Offices.

(f) Working with customers

Participation officers help to develop work with tenants' associations on council estates. Space is sometimes provided for community use. Tenants' groups are encouraged to form Management Co-ops on estates, e.g. Pavilion Co-op in Erdington. So far three have been established.

(g) Working with housing associations and the private sector

Land and/or loans are made available to housing associations. From 1982–1987 over 1,800 new or improved dwellings have been provided via City funding.

Urban renewal

5.48 The Environmental Services Department's Urban Renewal Division has responsibility for upgrading the private housing stock in the inner city. It has a 1987/88 budget of £39 million. It aims to improve houses and their environment and encourage public participation. Housing Action Areas and General Improvement Areas, as well as improvement grants and 'enveloping' (exterior repair and improvement works) have been used. Over 19,000 houses have been improved in this way. The local environment is also a focus of concern in many schemes where road and pavement improvements are made. With limited public resources, in future greater private sector involvement or personal household expenditure, will be necessary to improve older private housing. The Urban Renewal Division hopes to develop a community-based strategy — drawing on community views about the future, and employing, where possible, local residents, local firms and assisting the creation of new local firms to supply materials and labour. Grants have also been made available for improvement and repair to houses in multiple occupation.

5.49 From a Residents' Association perspective in the Aston area the Urban Renewal Division has been praised as 'streets ahead of other departments in cutting red-tape and getting things done, and setting up a proper system of consultation'. There has been good co-operation between residents and officials. Nevertheless there were areas of criticism. People felt that they had no real say in how money was spent. Residents were often not consulted in advance about major schemes. Much of the policy is seen still to create a dependency attitude, while the Residents' Association wants to encourage personal responsibility for repair and maintenance of homes. Residents often felt high prices seemed to be paid for what residents sometimes felt was shoddy work. Residents were not consulted about prices or the contractor who did the work though many were required to pay a proportion of the costs. The local Project Team Leader was not accessible and was not based in a local office. The overall impression within the Aston project area was one of mutual respect between local officers and residents, as was the case in Saltley.

Housing legislation

5.50 Current government housing legislation will have a profound effect on the future of housing in Urban Priority Areas. The role of the local authority will not be as a provider of housing but as a strategic housing planning body. The proposals will change the nature of council housing. The changes include the following:
— changes to the Housing Benefit system;
— means testing and targeting of house renovation grants;
— introducing competition and tendering for services traditionally carried out by council direct labour;
— a right for council tenants to opt for another landlord such as a housing association, tenant co-operative, private company or retain the City Council as landlord;
— Housing Action Trusts to take over run-down council estates and improve them;
— outlawing rate fund contributions to the Housing Revenue Account, thus making the housing service a self-financing trading account;
— encouraging private sector housing for rent at a reasonable rate of return on capital which will approximately double or triple many existing rents;
— reducing subsidy to housing associations and encouraging private sector investment.

The future of low income housing

5.51 These factors lead to concern about the future provision of housing for those on low income. Housing associations are concerned that private funding will act against provision in

inner city 'stress' areas because they will not be good areas for private investment. The pressure to use private finance could result in the present Housing Corporation's priority allocations to inner cities being diminished. It will also bring significantly higher rent levels. Local authority house building and finance to housing associations could cease. There is fear that government policy will mean:
— a continuing lack of sufficient rented dwellings for those in need;
— a programme of building new rented homes inadequate to meet the need in Birmingham;
— private sector contribution being unlikely to provide sufficient dwellings to meet the demand at a level of rent those in need can afford to pay, especially in the short-term.

Housing associations

5.52   Housing associations have played a growing part, particularly since the late 1960s, in the provision of accommodation for many people in Urban Priority Areas. They have provided a degree of much needed housing improvement in the older housing areas, as well as catering for the needs of many special groups, e.g. hostel accommodation. Often this work is carried out in consultation or collaboration with other agencies. Increasingly the housing associations are having to seek out private sector financing for schemes. They have had some degree of success in this, but some associations are concerned about their capacity to continue to provide decent housing for low-income, vulnerable groups in the City.

The importance of inner city housing

5.53   We must point out a dilemma of inner city policy in relation to housing. There are some doubts whether business will be able or willing to lead a regeneration of jobs in industry in the inner city (see 5.19 to 5.36 above). Most attractive industrial locations are on new open sites near motorway junctions. House building and improvement can produce more employment for local labour. Shops, offices and local services may also provide local employment opportunities. Regeneration in the medium term may be best achieved through new house building, refurbishment of older housing and environmental improvement. This strategy has an important part to play. The 1987 Unitary Plan Review for the West Midlands suggests here is a viable route for inner city regeneration. This has been agreed by the government. In relation to outer estates, Priority Estate Project schemes suggest that estate improvement using local labour provides a greater sense of local community confidence. Improvements to immediate residential surroundings, if properly serviced and maintained, produce a positive and concerned response from residents. Yet local authorities and housing associations may have to reduce expenditure in this field in an attempt to restrict rent increases.

(e) Education

Introduction

5.54 In this section we are primarily concerned with the schools education service. Birmingham's Education Service in its main provision consists of 26 nursery schools and 334 primary schools catering for 96,500 pupils; 88 secondary schools (including four sixth form colleges) which have just over 71,000 pupils; 9 colleges of further education, including the College of Food and Domestic Arts and Bournville College of Art and the City of Birmingham Polytechnic. There are amongst the City's schools 31 Church of England Schools and 66 Roman Catholic schools. These church schools number some 20 per cent of all schools in the City. Representatives of the churches sit on the Education Committee.

5.55 In 1983, declining pupil numbers led to a major reorganization of secondary schools with Sixth Forms in relatively few schools and with the creation of three new sixth form colleges. Strong resistance from governors, parents and staff makes it difficult to close schools but there is still over-provision of places, with the number of 16 year olds in the City expected to fall from over 15,000 in 1986 to just over 11,000 in 1990. There has also been reorganization of the provision in colleges of further education in response to the decline in apprenticeship schemes, unemployment and new technology. Falling rolls have posed, and continue to pose, immense problems of management. The decline in numbers is not even across the City and in some Urban Priority Areas there is pressure on available nursery and primary school places.

Staffing

5.56 Against a background of government spending curbs, Birmingham has reduced teacher numbers in line with pupil numbers. It introduced an early retirement scheme, and used more temporary contracts, a procedure which poses problems of continuity. Its reluctance to employ new staff has increased shortages in some specialist areas. In addition, the end of each academic year has seen massive staff redeployment which is difficult to manage at school level and has led to teachers being placed in inappropriate posts and to severe difficulties in maintaining the effective teaching of a broad and balanced curriculum.

5.57   Whilst the pupil–teacher ratios in the City are said to be near the national average, the figures can be misleading. A recent report by Her Majesty's Inspectors of Schools on Broadway School, an inner city school serving Aston and Handsworth, points out the although the overall pupil–teacher ratio apparently compares favourably with the national average, when the basis of that comparison is examined it is unfavourable and the school is only 'adequately' staffed. In addition, the low level of ancillary support means that some tasks are added to the load borne by the teachers.

5.58   Suitably qualified cover for maternity leave and long-term staff absence is often difficult to find and the Mobile Supply Teams are often over-stretched. Some schools have been able to recruit their own temporary replacements but others have found it more difficult. The effects on Urban Priority Area schools tend to be greater because they find it harder to attract staff.

5.59   The new arrangements for the in-service training of teachers and for the cover of short temporary staff absence have dramatically increased the use of relief teachers who are not part of the staff of the school. Not only has this used more central administrative time, but finding such teachers has placed considerable additional strains on schools. Again, the greater burdens are likely to be in the Urban Priority Area schools. The system of using relief teachers can have a detrimental effect on a school's ethos and on pupil learning because such teachers are not part of the school and because at the heart of effective teaching is a personal relationship between a teacher and a group of pupils. Where the school cannot find relief teachers to work regularly in the school, the effects are worst.

Expenditure

5.60   By comparison with other local authorities, Birmingham's expenditure on education has been below average since 1982/83. Budgets for teaching equipment, books and materials are low. This is reflected in capitation rates, so that in 1986 £15.9 per pupil was spent on equipment, tools and materials for primary school children, compared with a national average of £26.6. For secondary pupils the figure was £33.5 compared with £50.8 nationally. In the Urban Priority Areas lower private contributions from local communities to school budgets serve to reinforce disparities between more affluent and less affluent areas.

5.61   There are major problems of repair and maintenance and there is a general decline in the condition of the Education Department's buildings. This is especially acute in the inner city where 24.6 per cent of primary schools and 16.3 per cent of secondary schools were built before 1903 compared with 13.1 per cent and 7 per cent for Birmingham schools as a whole. Her Majesty's Inspectors of Schools have commented upon the poor condition of some schools, and have drawn attention to the poor state of cleanliness and possible health and safety hazards. During 1986/87, £9 million was made available for the repair and maintenance of city schools and colleges. A report by the City Engineer shows the need for £19 million to be spent on essential work.

5.62   Inner City Partnership resources are used to support the education service in the inner city. In 1986/87, 157 projects costing £0.765 million were funded. Much of the provision was for the under-fives and their parents and included the provision of parent/community rooms at schools and nurseries. Nevertheless, a report by the Handsworth and Aston Steering Committee of Head-teachers argues that education in the inner city is underfunded and understaffed and many outer Urban Priority Area schools face similar problems without any additional resources.

5.63   The City has some 600 posts, mainly in education, funded under Section 11 of the 1966 Local Government Act making special provision for the needs of Commonwealth immigrants. There is feeling in some sections of the leadership of the ethnic minority communities and elsewhere that this money is not always used in the most appropriate way.

Curriculum

5.64   Over the last decade or so there has been mounting criticism of state education and claims of declining standards and of irre-levant, theory-bound curricula. In August, 1986, Birmingham

Education Service published its Draft Curriculum Statement. It speaks of access to education as a basic right and of the responsibility of the Local Education Authority, as far as is possible, to ensure that its schools and colleges satisfy the needs and aspirations of all.

5.65   In September 1983, Birmingham was one of 14 LEAs to be in at the start of the Manpower Services Commission's Technical and Vocational Education Initiative (TVEI). This was to encourage practical, technical and vocational education. It was to be a five year pilot project. The work in the eight pilot schools and in the colleges involved has included a greater involvement of industry and commerce in the educational process, more relevant course content, a greater use of modern technology, a higher profile for careers education, the use of self-assessment techniques and negotiated learning routes and teaching styles which have encouraged greater maturity and self-esteem.

5.66   Now, as the pilot project draws to a close, the additional staffing resources are expected to be drawn out of the pilot institutions and it is unlikely that the programmes which have been developed will be sustained. Birmingham is bidding for inclusion in the TVEI Extension Scheme but the resources available at the level of the individual school or college do not compare with those available at the pilot stage and are unlikely to have anything like the same impact. At the same time it is difficult to see how the loss in the pilot schools is going to contribute to a wider gain. Outside of the TVEI programme other schools have been trying to go the same way but have been frustrated through inadequate resourcing.

5.67   The MSC style of funding sharply defined objectives, within its own priorities, has much to commend it. The pattern of funding developments which are not sustained because the Local Authority cannot or does not take on the additional costs once the money runs out is deficient. The history of curriculum development gives the lie to the notion that developments will continue once the development resources are withdrawn.

5.68   The move to establish City Technology Colleges must not lead to the illusion that sufficient is being done for technical and practical education. Such education provides a dimension to the curriculum that is needed for all, but in any competition for places it is children in Urban Priority Areas who are most likely to be disadvantaged. We welcome the creation of 'compacts' between schools and local firms. These are special relationships between industry and particular schools which encourage work experience, industry/school links, and lead to jobs for school-leavers attaining a required level of education.

Religious Education

5.69 Birmingham has a Standing Advisory Council on Religious Education (SACRE) which includes representatives from the Birmingham Council of Christian Churches and from Christian denominations not represented there as well as representatives of other faiths. Under the guidance of this SACRE, Birmingham produced, in 1975, its Agreed Syllabus and the handbook 'Living Together', which was adopted as a model by other local authorities.

5.70 The subject continues to present schools with difficulties. Well qualified teachers are difficult to find and some members of Christian religious groups are uncomfortable with the time and emphasis given to other faiths. Nevertheless, the Commission believes in the central importance of this subject area. Under recent reorganization, the Local Authority lost its specialist Adviser for Religious Education and the post was combined with Personal, Social and Moral Education. SACRE was not consulted about this change and has pressed for the reinstatement of the specialist post. A recent independent report by consultants from the University of Birmingham supports this and calls for the expansion of the advisory service for Religious Education.

GCSE

5.71 The Commission welcomes the educational objectives of the new GCSE examinations but it is clear that the introduction of this exam has not been matched by adequate staffing or materials. There is anxiety that time and money will be taken from the lower secondary school years to deliver the new system.

5.72 Children of middle-class parents did significantly better than their working-class peers in the old 'O' level system and it is feared that the new courses, with their stress on continuous assessment and project work, will widen this gap. Pupils with reference books and word processors and having parents with skills in school subject areas are likely to be significantly advantaged. Under a norm referencing system, which compares one with another, this is even more exaggerated.

The Multi-ethnic context

5.73   About 30 per cent, or 60,000 young people within the Birmingham education systems, are from Afro-Caribbean or Asian ethnic minority communities. In 1978 the City formally adopted a policy of multi-cultural education. The City's Race Relations Unit finds evidence of good multicultural educational practice especially in some inner city schools but it believes that in many predominantly white schools the policy has had little impact. It argues the need for a greater stress on anti-racist education and for the service to reflect more uniformly the City's commitment to challenge racism by correcting misunderstanding, myth and stereotypes and to removing practices and procedures which deny equality of opportunity. The issues which arise are debated nationally as well as locally and feelings run high in communities which feel powerless and on the margins of society.

5.74   In areas with a high concentration of Asian and Afro-Caribbean population there are increasing numbers of schools with nearly 95 per cent of pupils from these ethnic groups. Some schools draw most of their pupils from a single ethnic minority community. There is evidence to suggest that these schools are not selected by parents of white children because they do not want their children to be in a school where they are in a minority. This particularly involves schools serving the inner city. Once parents who can afford to do so send their children to schools outside the area, the standing and morale of the local school is affected and its reputation has little to do with the quality of its academic work. This is an area of major concern for Birmingham. Church schools are often popular with Asian parents.

5.75   There is continuing anxiety about the educational attainments of pupils of Afro-Caribbean descent and in the communities themselves the feeling is still expressed that teachers do not expect their children to be academic. A Birmingham Commission for Racial Equality survey of 1985 found that pupils who were primarily of Afro-Caribbean origin were four times more likely to be placed in school suspension units and six times more likely to be suspended under the age of 15 than white pupils. Since then the Education Authority has revised its suspension procedures and this has resulted in fewer cases going through formal procedures, although there remains a

fear that informal procedures still affect a disproportionately high
number of these pupils.

5.76   Asian groups argue strongly for single-sex schools, particularly
for their girls, and press for a curriculum which encourages
their religion and their culture. At both city and local level
much remains to be done in constructively bringing together the
Education Service and the different communities it serves.

5.77   On school governing bodies, Asian and Afro-Caribbean
parents are under-represented, although some schools have
made great efforts to encourage participation. Under new
legislation, the powers of governing bodies are strengthened and there
is opportunity for greater involvement in the work of schools and
colleges. The shortage of teachers from Asian and Afro-Caribbean
background is a matter of concern to the Local Authority. Of those who
are in post, many work in specialist areas such as the Multi-Cultural
Support Services and relatively few are employed above the basic scale.

5.78   Community language provision exists in some schools although
the range of languages represented in Birmingham is large
and the level of support for pupils whose mother tongue is not
English tends to be inadequate. This reflects both the difficulty of
recruiting adequately trained staff for this specialist work and also the
result of financial limitations.
The Bullock Report fuses the role of language in learning and in child
development. It identifies the centrality of language in the cognitive and
affective development of children. The implications for schools are
clear. Staff need to share the languages and cultures of their pupils if
there is to be any effective learning and development of pupils'
experiences. The engagement of bi-lingual staff is a priority issue for
schools with a predominantly bi-lingual population if they are to be in a
position to deliver quality education.

Youth Employment and Continuing Education

5.79   Trends in employment and training for young people very
much affect the destination of school leavers. YTS is now the
main destination of 16 year old leavers and it is clear that the
majority of employers are not eager to recruit at this age but prefer to
take people who possess skills and/or experience enabling them to
contribute quickly to the production of goods and services. Less than
one third of the jobs entered offer skill training whilst at the same time

there is a shortage of appropriately qualified recruits to technician level training and many young people do not see jobs in engineering and manufacturing as attractive options. These skill shortages will have implications for economic growth especially in manufacturing industry. The need continues for positive images of industry in education.

5.80   The Local Education Authority is currently discussing collaborative ventures with industry through which the Authority, schools and industrialists will work out together a set of mutual commitments aimed at meeting the needs of learners and increasing mutual understanding. The project includes resourcing from industry, support for industrialists seeking to learn more of the education system, establishing positive attitudes towards industry and commerce, and a commitment by schools to tackle some of the anxieties expressed by industrialists.

5.81   Ethnic minority groups equally or better qualified than whites at the lower educational levels find it more difficult to secure employment and the Commission for Racial Equality has argued that there is racial discrimination within the YTS system. Even with higher qualifications many ethnic minority graduates experience greater difficulty in obtaining employment, suffer longer unemployment periods and often settle for jobs inferior to their qualifications.

5.82   At a time when education attainment levels are improving, many young people are taking work which is at a lower level than one would expect, given their educational qualifications. At the same time, pupils in Birmingham leave school with lower levels of examination qualifications than nationally and, as in the West Midlands as a whole, few stay on to take 'A' levels. At a time of high, though declining, unemployment, this is disadvantageous to the pupils of Birmingham.

5.83   Over the period 1984–1986 the proportion of Fifth Year pupils continuing in full time education has been consistent at about 36 per cent. Some young people pursue 'O' and 'A' level courses where they have limited chances of success and despite the publication of a 'Beyond 16' booklet more remains to be done to give adequate guidance about the full range of courses available at this stage.

5.84   For 16 year olds not going on into full time education, YTS is the major option. In certain industries (e.g. building and motor vehicles) YTS has virtually become the only way of gaining access to craft level training. 4,811 of Birmingham's 16 year olds entered YTS in 1986 (nearly 33 per cent of the school leavers). This was a 7 per cent drop over 1985. 1986 saw the first intake into the new two year YTS and anecdotal evidence suggests that the longer period deterred some. A more significant reason, given by young people themselves, is the low rate of allowance which has increased very little over the last seven years. Generally, enough YTS places were available to meet demand, except in catering and motor vehicle work. Since 1983, YTS has shifted away from a broader development role to a much more specific job training programme so that the scheme does not easily accommodate the opportunity to sample a variety of work areas, but on the other hand produces less superficial job experience and training.

Community education

5.85   Some schools are 'dual use': they have facilities provided by the Recreation and Community Services Department and are managed by them at evenings and weekends. The dual management system can lead to tensions. The Commission considers that an effective community education policy awaits development and that this is essential in Urban Priority Areas where it is central to community involvement and enhanced community well-being.

Conclusion

5.86   There can be little doubt that in Education we are looking at an inadequately resourced service. It is clear that it faces many challenges which are sharply focused in the Urban Priority Areas. There is much frustration at all levels in the Service over reports and legislation which set out visions of a better future without providing the resources for change. Often, the lack of finance means that the changes concentrate only on the ways in which people work. Whilst the Commission acknowledges the need for efficiency, it recognizes that human change needs resources — in particular, adequate retraining time.

(f) **Social Care**

5.87   Social care is attempting to meet the needs of individuals and communities in a total context. It is not a question therefore of concern only to the Social Services Department, for social care includes health and medical care, education, housing, poverty and unemployment. Private and voluntary organizations, including the churches are also essential participants in the provision of social care. Above all social care often and most naturally falls primarily upon the family unit and upon relatives, friends and neighbours. Many agency initiatives provide respite for these 'natural carers'.

5.88   Birmingham Social Services Department, already giving help to many thousands, is experiencing increasing demand for its services. The Department's policy of decentralizing its services is a response to growing demand and to the need to target resources on areas of intense deprivation, particularly those to be found on some outer estates and in the inner city. Responses to these growing needs have been curtailed through financial restriction.

Children and families

5.89   About 1 per cent of Birmingham's children are in the statutory care of the City Council's childrens' homes or with foster parents. Recently the Social Services Department has been able to improve its day care facilities for pre-school children in response to a major increase in the younger child population. Social Services provide 1,500 day care places, child minders provide 3,200 places and the voluntary, church and informal groups provide further significant facilities. A vital issue in assisting early education is whether nursery provision exists in sufficient quantity, flexibility and quality to make any real impact on the lives of young children and their parents living in Urban Priority Areas. Birmingham makes statutory provision for pre-school children. Much of the Inner City Partnership resources are used to provide facilities for the under 5s and their parents. The Education Authority provides 32 pre-school workers funded under Section 11 (see 5.63) working in Urban Priority Area schools, all with flourishing play groups. In addition there were 5,963 children in nursery schools and classes in 1987. Birmingham churches have some very innovative schemes to meet the needs of pre-school children. There is nevertheless a need for more nursery places, better funding and better environmental conditions for staff and pupils. Play centres, both statutory and voluntary, play a significant role here. Social Services concern to protect children from risks of abuse can produce stressful situations for all involved. Child protection requires inter-agency co-ordination and, especially with regard to ethnic minority groups, is increasingly seen as requiring specialist, therapeutic skills. A scheme involving police, probation and social services now monitors the Juvenile Justice System to investigate ways of reducing juvenile crime.

The elderly

5.90 About 3 per cent of those aged 75 or over live in residential homes run by the Social Services Department (over 2,000 places in 43 homes). The private and voluntary sectors also increasingly provide residential accommodation for the elderly. The Social Services Department regulates and inspects standards in private and voluntary sector residential homes. Wherever possible non-institutionalized forms of care are preferred and the conversion of large residential homes into smaller units continues. Such conversions and that form of care are expensive.

5.91 In recent years the emphasis has been on care of the elderly in the community, enabling them to continue to live in their own homes. About 25 per cent of the over 75s benefit from the home help service (19,500 people in 1987) and each year some 10,000 elderly people are provided with aids to living or housing adaptations to make life easier and assist independence. The task of home helps has been broadened to wider caring to meet the needs of elderly people better. A scheme to provide intensive home help and other services to the elderly in a tower block (Manton House) is being evaluated. Other services include the provision of over 1 million meals per year to elderly people in their own homes or through luncheon clubs. Over 15,000 free travel passes are issued to Birmingham pensioners each year. Community care of the elderly is under-resourced. Elderly people will be particularly affected by changes in the Supplementary Benefits system (see 5.17, 5.18). The number of very elderly people (aged over 85 years) in the City is increasing rapidly. In 1987 there were about 12,250 such people, but by 1995 it is expected that the number will be 15,250. This will place increasing demands upon over-stretched and under-resourced services which the Local Authority, by itself, is unable to meet. The work done by Birmingham Council for Old People and Age-Concern/ Visiting Service for Old People is invaluable and will become increasingly important. The Griffiths Report on community care and the Wagner Report on residential care are both important recent documents which attempt to improve service quality.

Mentally ill and mentally handicapped

5.92 Services for the mentally handicapped and mentally ill are the subject of Birmingham's Community Care Special Action Project, begun in 1987, which aims to bring together City departments and health authorities to promote a more co-ordinated approach to this aspect of community care, following criticisms of the City's services for the mentally ill. There is great need of social support for mentally handicapped people who have previously been in institutions. Increasing numbers of the mentally handicapped now live independently in the community supported by care workers. Voluntary organizations include the Elfrida Rathbone Society working with young people by providing employment, housing and recreation facilities. As young people leave the City's special schools they will require extra day-care places. The questions of appropriate care and support in the community is the subject of a national enquiry, the Griffiths Report.

5.93   Services for the mentally ill are the priority for Social Services bids for Inner City Partnership funding over the next few years, to tackle the high level of mental health difficulties experienced by people living in inner city Urban Priority Areas. Three Social Services districts in the City have collaborated in a study of circumstances and numbers of admissions or re-admissions, voluntary or compulsory, of mentally ill people to hospital. Early results suggest community-based alternatives to hospital admissions are often inadequately considered. Local provision of services for the mentally ill by District Health Authorities is now being emphasized, rather than services based on large psychiatric hospitals. It is necessary to provide services to mentally ill people living in the community. Often they are marginalized in the labour market as well as suffering social deprivation. Day and residential services require close collaboration between health and social services. The pioneering Community Mental Health Centre at Underwood Road shows the importance of day-care services.

The physically handicapped

5.94   Demand for services for physically handicapped people far outstrips resources. In addition to home-based services, such as home helps and meals on wheels, there are about 400 day-care places and also specialist residential accommodation for 91 people. The number of physically handicapped people in the community will continue to rise. This, together with the Disabled Persons' Act of 1986 with its resource implications and the new obligations upon local authorities, will increase pressure on the service. Parts of the Act are due for implementation in 1987/88. There is a national shortage of occupational therapists — a 22 per cent shortfall nationally. This leads to unacceptable delays in response to non-urgent requests for help. The service operates on the basis of response to requests rather than on the basis of full provision for needs throughout the City. This may act against the interests of Urban Priority Area residents.

5.95 Care services face difficulties over culture and language amongst ethnic minority groups. Ethnic minority communities draw particular attention to the need for nursery schools and for day care for young children. Voluntary groups provide much of this service and use volunteers as well as paid part-time help e.g. Olive Branch Community Centre day nursery where mothers from different ethnic minority communities provide a high quality of nursery care assisted by MSC funding. Day centres and residential homes for the elderly often increase the sense of loneliness and isolation felt by Afro-Caribbean and Asian people. We also found that others such as Polish immigrants felt isolated when not with people of their own background and language. Sensitive placements and creation of small units within larger residential homes for special groups is of great help. There is now a number of hostels and refuges run specifically for Asian or Afro-Caribbean women.

Funding problems

5.96 The Social Services Committee of the City Council has supported a growing range of voluntary activity in the City in line with its general concern for social care, either from Inner City Partnership provision or out of its mainstream funding. Other Council committees also support the voluntary sector. As we shall see in Section (g) (5.98–5.107), the Recreation and Community Services Committee plays a significant part in encouraging community development and voluntary sector initiatives. In 1988 the voluntary sector in Birmingham faces a major funding crisis, of which funding from Social Services is one important element. Time-expired projects under the Inner City Partnership add to this problem since they cannot be supported solely from the Social Services Committee mainstream funding. Needs continue to expand whilst the financial resources contract.

Inter-agency co-operation

5.97 There is a need for further development of co-ordination of social care projects between different caring authorities and co-operation with the voluntary and private sectors, including the churches. Such co-ordination is exemplified by the opening of a social and recreational centre for the mentally ill at Soho Hill, Handsworth. It offers wide facilities for some 200 people a week in developing life skills and restoring personal confidence. The centre is actively supported by a range of community, ethnic minority and voluntary groups. This is a good example of co-ordinated and co-operative social support and care which is increasingly important in Urban Priority Areas.

(g) Recreation, Leisure and Community Development

Introduction

5.98 Ready access to recreation and leisure facilities by residents of Urban Priority Areas is very important. Facilities are provided by bodies in the private, public and voluntary sectors. The range of facilities is enormous and includes sports, education, music, drama, parks, festivals, libraries and a variety of commercial facilities provided for those who wish to participate. Access depends not only on geographical distance but also on the cost. The Recreation and Community Services Department divides the City into 12 areas which are co-terminous with parliamentary constituencies. Each area has its own manager (who is usually responsible for all the Department's facilities) and who is supported by a team of specialists including Community Development Officers, Community Recreation Officers, Youth Officers and Adult Education Officers. This Department is responsible for the Youth Service, elsewhere often run by Education Departments. It shares with the Education Department responsibility for Adult Education. The City Council stresses the importance of community development as a process of involving local people, which is seen to be just as important as the outcome of a particular project. We believe this is essential if people are to have dignity and power.

The voluntary youth organizations

5.99 Birmingham has a long tradition of voluntary youth provision in which the Churches have played a significant part. The Birmingham Council for Voluntary Youth Services represents approximately 30 City-wide youth organizations and estimates that its constituency is in contact with 50,000 young people. The principal point of contact for the voluntary youth sector is via the Recreation and Community Services Department but many youth organizations receive no City funding while others with a specialist remit receive funding from Education, Social Services or Housing. The term 'youth organization' is often misleading as many deal with those down to the age of 5 and are often involved in play work.

The Birmingham Association of Youth Clubs is one of the principal youth organizations, providing facilities to 146 Youth Clubs including regular mailings, training facilities and organizational support on administrative or legal affairs. There are many youth clubs in Urban Priority Areas amongst its membership. Through the Birmingham Council of Christian Churches the Youth Officers of the denominations piloted an interdenominational training course for voluntary youth leaders. A number of youth organizations sponsor detached youth work projects, including the Church of England Children's Society and Barnardo's. 'Drugline' is involved in counselling work with young drug takers. In 1987, 'International Year of Shelter for the Homeless', the voluntary sector produced an information booklet for those leaving home, entitled 'Moving Out'. In addition St. Basil's in conjunction with the City have produced a fact sheet on young people and homelessness for clergy and other professionals.

Youth work with ethnic minorities

5.100   Whilst there are an increasing number of Afro-Caribbean and Asian young people who are separating themselves from their cultural, historical and religious roots and are subject to the effects of racism, there are many who derive strength, identity and hope from their roots. Provision must be made available to them if they are to have a stake in this society. The level of alienation felt by young black and Asian people must not be ignored and concerted action needs to be taken. This problem affects the way those with power, whether teachers, clergy, youth workers, police or other professionals relate to young black and Asian citizens. Some efforts are being made, for example, the Youth Panel of the Birmingham Community Relations Council is a voice for ethnic minority youth groups at the City level. A number of significant projects have been established by ethnic communities themselves. The Sikh Youth Service, based in Handsworth, has had a full-time worker since 1983 and provides advice and information, promotes Sikh culture and identity and co-ordinates activities for young people. The Court Workers Project is now administered by the Probation Service but it developed from concerns in the late 1970s arising from meetings between St. Basil's Centre, the Birmingham Council of Christian Churches and leaders of the Black-led churches. Other significant projects are the United Evangelical Project (sponsored by a number of Black-led churches), the Link House for Asian Girls, the Handsworth Cultural Centre and 'CAVE' (Cultural and Village Entertainment) run by the Probation Service.

Community development

5.101   There is close collaboration between the Recreation and
Community Services Department and the voluntary sector,
including churches and church based organizations. The Area
Community Development Officers act in an advisory capacity and offer
professional advice. Grants are made to voluntary sector schemes
through a variety of funding sources including Community Chest and
the Inner City Partnership. In 1987/1988 £1.8m was available for
community groups. Funding is available for churches to make their
premises suitable for wider community use (see Chapter 4).

Youth and play policies

5.102   In March 1986 the City Council adopted a Policy for Youth
Work in Birmingham. In the same year Area Youth Councils
were formed together with the City-wide Birmingham Young
People's Council — the work of these is patchy. They try to encourage
young people to have leadership roles in the organization, running and
development of the Youth Service. The Youth Service is increasing the
arts content of its programme. There is a special training scheme for
youth and community workers at Westhill College which is aimed at
women and ethnic minorities. The City's training facilities at the
Stainsby Centre in Hockley are widely used by the voluntary sector.
The Council approved a Play Policy in 1987: as with youth work the
voluntary sector makes significant contributions to play work, e.g. St.
Martin's Centre in Highgate, and Hockley Flyover Adventure Playground (which is involved in latchkey work and has undertaken work
on ethnic minority play provision). There are 14 City play centres,
mainly sited in parks. While welcoming these policy statements there is
concern, particularly amongst the voluntary sector that they cannot be
operated effectively without a major reallocation of resources. The
policies are particularly important in relation to anti-racism and anti-
sexism.

Public use of school buildings

5.103   The City has pursued a policy of opening school buildings for
wider community use (a dual use policy). This provision is
being enhanced by the construction of three sports halls on the
sites of Shenley, Marsh Hill and Colmers Farm Schools. When
complete they will extend the network of dual use sites and leisure

centres. Current government plans mean that local authority leisure
centres will have to be put out to competitive contract for their
management. This has implications for pricing and wider community
use. We urge that such privatization measures should not restrict access
by lower income groups nor hinder the further development of such
facilities in Urban Priority Areas.

Community recreation associations

5.104   In order to encourage community involvement in the manage-
ment of facilities a number of Community Recreation Associ-
ations have been formed. One example is the Magnet Centre in
Erdington which has been created by a partnership between the City
Council and the West Midland Greek Cypriot Association. It purchased
the Magnet Centre from GEC in 1984, supported by grants from the
West Midlands County Council and from the Inner City Partnership
Programme.

Sports

5.105   A regional sports strategy was developed in the early 1980s by
the West Midlands Council for Sport and Recreation. This
identified the sports needs of young people (13–24 years), the
middle aged (45–59) and women. It also laid emphasis on developing
local sports leadership and developing facilities and programmes to
promote competitive sporting excellence. The basic aim of the strategy
was to encourage a much wider participation in sports by the
population as a whole. The probation service and the police are also
active in providing sports facilities as are commercial interests and the
voluntary sector.

Recreation and community projects

5.106   The Saltley Sports Hall, opened in 1987, is an example of
Inner City Partnership resources being used to fund recreation
and leisure projects and offers a variety of activities. Martial
arts, ballet, badminton and football are catered for while community
rooms offer facilities for the elderly, the unemployed and others. Such a
centre will be subject to new competitive tendering legislation.
Sparkhill library's programme of arts and social courses designed for
the multi-cultural needs of the area, led by local community representa-

tives is another example of imaginative response to community needs. The old BSA site in the inner city now provides ambitious and extensive recreational facilities. The site was reclaimed at a cost of £1.5 million and is leased to the Ackers Trust, a voluntary body, which manages and maintains the site. It provides adventurous outdoor activities within an inner city environment. The site has a nature reserve along the River Cole, canoeing and narrow boats on the Grand Union Canal, a free-standing climbing wall for supervised mountain climbing instruction and a dry ski slope. A local brewery helped to refurbish the clubhouse.

Conclusion

5.107 Community Forum, the principal citywide body of Tenants and Residents Associations, strongly supported the concept of community education as providing the way forward on community development. We would endorse this approach. We have found that outer estates are relatively neglected in this process and that resources are more readily available in the inner city — but much remains to be done at a very local level, e.g. adequate youth/community facilities on the Wyrley Birch Estate. Finally, adequate provision will only be attained by action cutting across the public, private and voluntary sectors and by individuals and communities taking action.

(h) **Order and Law**

Introduction

5.108 We give our title as order and law, not law and order, simply because law is the servant of order but does not produce it. Order in our communal life is not something bestowed on us or even maintained by the police or the courts. Order is consent to commonly accepted aims, aspirations and concerns of society. In such a situation law helps to regulate that order and to define the rights and duties of individuals and groups. Where there is serious disorder, common consent has broken down. Law then has a different function, to contain, prevent or punish manifestations of that disorder.

5.109 When there is disorder society needs to address itself dispassionately to the roots of that disorder, to listen to those who perceive themselves as oppressed or discriminated against. But it is not sufficient merely to hear the voice of the oppressed on consultative bodies or liaison groups — practical and legal action should be taken to meet injustices. Laws which seek to regulate conduct in such areas as race and sex discrimination always recognize a moral imperative. Law cannot change people's hearts and attitudes. Better laws do not, by themselves, create a moral society.

5.110 Law is fundamentally to do with justice, and all human laws and the human understanding of justice which laws express, are ultimately to be measured against God's justice which has a particular concern for 'prisoners and captives', and with all others whose social position renders them weak and vulnerable (see Chapter 6). In this respect we acknowledge the work of many advice and law centres, particularly in the inner city Urban Priority Areas. They are often underfunded and live with the constant possibility of closure.

5.111 Although we concentrate here upon aspects of order and law to which the police and the probation service relate, it is necessary to have this wider perspective always in mind. The role of the police in the multi-cultural setting of Birmingham is not easy. Most citizens are law abiding and support the difficult but necessary work of the police. Birmingham's police and probation services are part of a larger service organized on the geographical area of the former West Midlands County Council. Both services are decentralized at operational level.

(i) *Police service*

Key themes

5.112 The police identify their four key operational concerns as crime, public order, community relations and traffic.

5.113 In 1986 West Midlands recorded criminal offences increased by 10.3 per cent to 255,540. This was the steepest rise since 1982. In 1986 the detection rate fell by 0.7 per cent to 29.3 per cent. In 1987 offences increased by 1 per cent but there was a higher detection rate. It is not possible to identify what proportion of that improved detection rate was due to initiatives launched by the police themselves which encouraged the public to report matters which might otherwise have been ignored. In 1986 serious crimes did not increase and the detection rate of such crime has been maintained. Robbery and theft from the person has increased, often aggravated by the use of a weapon. Perpetrators do not discriminate in choice of victim nor, it seems, are they particularly deterred by the presence of other people.

Offences such as these involving violence account for only 2.9 per cent of total crime.

5.114 Dwelling house burglary has increased sharply and in 1986 represented some 32 per cent of recorded crimes. A number of initiatives have been targetted at this problem, e.g. Neighbourhood Watch, Business Watch, the Ladworth Project and several inner city crime reduction projects. These involve local communities as well as the police. Recent figures suggest that these schemes have had a significant impact on such crimes, especially within inner city Urban Priority Areas. Theft of motor vehicles and of property from vehicles has risen sharply, possibly because of the growing success of policing and other methods which have helped to prevent other crimes such as burglaries. A high priority is given to drug-related offences and the association between drug abuse and other areas of criminal activity is one of increasing concern. New posts for police officers to work in the area of child abuse have been created. This follows from a joint police/ social services working partly and demonstrates that many issues require an inter-agency approach if they are to be tackled effectively. The police are encouraging both a corporate inter-agency and local community approach to crime reduction.

Public order

5.115 Public order has been a particular priority of the police after the tragic disturbances in North Birmingham in 1985. Even minor outbursts of unreasonable behaviour can undermine the peacefulness of many people's lives. The problem exists in various forms. It can merely be a disturbance among loitering youths in public areas, or deliberate and organized larger scale violence. Various initiatives have been taken in an effort to utilize sport and other types of informal contact to bridge the gap between police and a local community. Drugs and drunkenness are often significant factors in disorder and violence. The police are active members of the Court Alcohol Committee and the Birmingham Alcohol Liaison Committee. Prostitution and its related activities cause problems in certain parts of the City. In Balsall Health and Moseley the police have often been prompted to take action by local residents and residents associations. Churches are concerned about these problems and a number of outreach projects and support for ex-prostitutes are organized. Maintaining order is not always easy. Police officers are frequently assaulted and abused when carrying out their duties. On average there are four assaults per day on the police, resulting in two officers being hospitalized each day.

Community links

5.116 The police increasingly direct attention to improving relations with and between the communities they serve. Serious attempts are made to understand the needs of particular groups and to develop greater mutual understanding with disaffected sections of society. The strategies used include training for police to develop their awareness of racial and social issues, and maintaining greater openness with the media. Involvement in police training by other agencies is essential. This should include the clergy, social workers and ethnic minority community representatives. A previous church input by the Rector of St. Martin's in the Bull Ring ended when he moved. We note that the Handsworth and Aston Forum of Churches is to be involved in aspects of the training programme. We welcome this but feel this initiative should be developed more widely. There has been a campaign to recruit police from ethnic minority communities. The West Midlands Police Force has one of the highest ratios of ethnic minority police officers of any police force at 2.1 per cent. Recent police intakes have been 11 per cent from ethnic minorities, divided equally between Asian and Afro-Caribbeans. The Police Force must reflect the ethnic composition of the West Midlands if it is to maintain credibility with many people.

Ethnic minority relations

5.117 The Commission was concerned to hear from Afro-Caribbean ethnic groups and others, such as the Handsworth and Aston Forum of Churches and the Birmingham Diocesan Council for Social Responsibility, that the relationship between police and some communities in the North of the City was not good. It was generally not the locally based police officers, who were specially trained and often sensitive to local issues, who caused concern, but rather the sudden introduction into an area of large numbers of police from outside when the police felt that order was under threat. The potential use of plastic bullets and the appearance of armoured vehicles, the sounding of sirens and close surveillance from a helicopter can increase tension and excitement in sensitive areas. It was not only young Afro-Caribbeans who expressed these views, but also a number of middle aged people, many of whom are members of Christian congregations and say they have experienced police harassment. From our discussions with the police we are aware that these issues also cause them concern. The police acknowledge stereotyping and unsatisfactory attitudes amongst some officers and some have been dismissed from the force because of racial bias.

5.118   The problems facing the police in Birmingham's Urban
Priority Areas are complex. The police are seen as representatives of authority and as such are often targets for generalized
resentments and frustrations. The West Midlands Police is financially
constrained but requires more police officers to discharge its responsibilities successfully. The recruitment of civilians to release more police
officers for operational duties has had some success but the serious
shortage of police officers remains.

Inter-agency co-operation

5.119   Over the last few years the police have made greater efforts to
co-operate with other agencies, both statutory and voluntary
bodies, and with the community. They are involved with the
City Council in developing a comprehensive strategy for crime
reduction in the City, especially within Urban Priority Areas. The
initiative aims to involve local communities themselves. The Ladworth
Project, covering Ladywood and Handsworth, involves the police, City
Council and voluntary organizations in helping to reduce crime. The
Inner City Partnership is funding a series of crime prevention projects
mainly in inner city Urban Priority Areas. The local Police Liaison
Committees play an important role though local people and the
Churches need to be better represented. There is regular contact
between the Community Liaison section of the police, the Chief
Constable and the Birmingham Council of Christian Churches. Local
Police Liaison Committees are often frustrating meetings. There is
sometimes a feeling that the voice of the community is not listened to.
Officers responsible for Community Liaison have achieved a lot in
creating positive relationships with the community, but there is unease
as many people feel that many sections of the Police Force regard them
as peripheral. Inter-agency co-operation is very necessary. Crime
prevention is now more emphasized as a significant element of policing
than in the past and new ways are being forged with local communities
and other agencies to ensure co-operative approaches to preventing
crime in both inner and outer Urban Priority Areas and elsewhere.

(ii) *Probation Service*

Introduction

5.120   The primary aims of the Probation Service are to provide social
reports on offenders and to assist magistrates and offenders.
The service also helps with community service, probation and
bail hostels, and with providing support to prisoners and their families

during and after imprisonment. Other forms of assistance are also provided in domestic and divorce courts. Officers work in collaboration with many statutory and voluntary organizations. By December 1986 some 5,000 offenders and their families were being supervised and assisted in Birmingham. About 55 per cent were subject to probation or community service orders. The great majority of the service's clients have been convicted on more than one occasion. In 1986 of all new community service orders on Birmingham offenders 91 per cent had one or more previous convictions and 33 per cent had 6 or more.

Social context

5.121   Many persistent offenders have multiple difficulties in their daily lives. The most frequent common factor is low income, which is usually associated with two or more of the following: unemployment (90 per cent of all new offenders in 1986 were unemployed), homelessness, frequent change of address, lack of stable relationships, debt, overcrowding, poor physical health, lack of social and/or employment skills, below average literacy and numeracy, dependents with similar problems, little or no practical support available from neighbours or other family members. Probation officers are daily witnesses to grinding poverty.

Social security benefits

5.122   Probation officers and social workers have been deeply concerned about the changes in both eligibility for and the level of state benefits over the last two years. These include:

(i) disqualification for voluntarily leaving employment extended from six to thirteen weeks;

(ii) no single payment for anyone who has not been on benefit for 12 months;

(iii) cutting back the value of furniture grants and their increasingly complex regulations.

Because of the many pressures on DHSS staff in local offices it takes longer for claims to be dealt with and queries sorted out. Probation officers are particularly anxious about vulnerable 16–25 year olds in relation to changes in social security provision implemented in April 1988.

Probation Service initiatives

5.123   Steps have been taken by the Probation Service to deal with these problems, including assistance with accommodation, encouraging social skills and self-confidence. It has supported projects like the Handsworth Cultural Centre, Birmingham Wheels, and the CAVE (Cultural and Village Entertainment). Much work is being done in collaboration with other agencies such as the Juvenile Liaison Panels with the police, the education service and social services. This has resulted in juveniles being dealt with other than by appearing in court, thus deferring or preventing the spiral of recurrent offences.

Inter-agency co-operation

5.124 The Probation Service strongly supports the need for greater inter-agency co-operation at community level and the need for effective inter-agency working in neighbourhoods. The Probation Service operates many such schemes throughout the City.

(iii) *Immigration*

5.125 A number of serious problems and issues emerge for immigrant communities as a result of the 1981 Nationality Act. By 31st December 1987 all those who did not already possess British citizenship had to register for citizenship. Many black people see the legislation as a slur imposed upon them and consider immigration control and monitoring is unacceptably intrusive and based on racism. Local authority agencies will lose confidence and credibility if they are perceived as exchanging private and confidential information about black people with the Home Office. The Birmingham Diocesan Council for Social Responsibility developed an advice service on nationality and citizenship matters and a fund was established to help people to pay the £60 registration fee before the end of 1987. The Birmingham Methodist District and the City Council also set up such funds as did some congregations. The work of the Birmingham Community Relations Council is·also important, as is that of the Citizens' Advice Bureau. Such citizenship issues make many long-established residents of the City feel insecure and discriminated against.

(i) **Health and Medical Care**

Introduction

5.126 We believe that people have a right to expect reasonable medical care in Birmingham irrespective of where they live, their social class, their immediate environment or their particular illness or disability. There has been growing concern about disparities in health and in the provision of medical care in cities. The Black Report addressed such issues as are reflected in Birmingham.

Health inequalities

5.127   The DHSS Report on 'Inequalities in Health', chaired by Sir Douglas Black in 1980, disclosed among other things that:

 (i) there are marked differences in mortality rates between occupational classes;
 (ii) long-standing illness is twice as common in lower class social groups as in professional groups;
 (iii) there was a widening gap between the health experience of unskilled and semi-skilled groups compared with professional groups over the 1960s and 1970s;
 (iv) there were inequalities in the utilization of medical services, especially of the preventive services, with severe under-utilization by the working classes;
 (v) differences in material living conditions is the most significant factor giving rise to differences in physical and mental health.

Other reports, including that of 1987 by the Health Education Council, confirm these findings.

Problems and financial restraint

5.128   Recent crises and public debate have revealed deficiencies and difficulties in the National Health Service in Birmingham. More money than ever before has been spent on the NHS, but alongside this fact must be set the greatly increased range of effective treatment now possible and a vastly wider vision of educative and preventive measures. Cuts in provision of services fall more heavily upon the poor of the Urban Priority Areas who are unable to afford private care, who compete inadequately for scarce services and who cannot opt out of long waiting lists.

5.129   The Central Birmingham Health Authority covers eight wards. In three of these, Nechells, Sparkbrook and Sparkhill, there is severe multiple deprivation. Sparkbrook is the most deprived of all the wards in the City. The major health care problems are much greater in these three inner city wards and inequalities and disparities are severe. A policy concentrated on health promotion and improved primary medical care would be likely to lead to a lessening of disparities and health improvements in the most deprived areas. Some 45 per cent of the population of the Authority is in the extremely deprived category, but the ability of the authority to shift resources is limited not only by overall restriction but also by its unique responsibilities as a major teaching and specialist hospital centre of national importance. It has a duty to provide these services for patients from the rest of the region. The allocation balance is being currently investigated. The Authority states that the RAWP formula (by which central government money is allocated to health authorities on a measure of need to spend) does not adequately account for the tasks which the Authority is expected to do and because of this, inequalities in health in Central Birmingham are unlikely to be removed. Indeed, in 1987/88 the funding of health services in the whole region and especially Birmingham came under severe pressure with closure of hospital beds, reduction of staff, long waiting lists and situations near to or at crisis point. South Birmingham Health Authority describes its situation as striving to provide services against the background of unprecedented resource constraints in both capital and revenue terms. This, coupled with a drive for efficiency and the re-orientation of service values to improve the quality of care, gives an indication of difficulties facing the South Birmingham Health Authority.

A picture of health

5.130   The 1987 report from the Central Birmingham Health Authority, 'A picture of health?', gives clear evidence of the links between poor health and social and economic deprivation. Unemployment, lower incomes, divorce and marriage breakdown, alcoholism, drug abuse, increasing proportions of very old people, one parent families, and poor housing (dampness, overcrowding, high rise flats, etc.) all contribute to poor health, depression, stress and tension. These conditions of illness are particularly associated with Urban Priority Areas. The physical and mental health of inner city residents is relatively poor, with the incidence of serious disease and death up to three times that of the outer wards of the City. The inner city is also characterized by a large proportion of young people under 15 years of age (28 per cent in 1981). Poor housing, poor job opportunities and poor health co-exist.

Ethnic minority groups

5.131   Men and women of the ethnic minority groups have made a great contribution to the work of the NHS over many years. This is very evident in Birmingham, both in the hospitals and in the community. Many of them and many other low-paid employees of the NHS live in the Urban Priority Areas and are suffering discouragement both in pressured work situations and poor living conditions at home. Health Authorities still face the challenge of developing appropriate provision for Afro-Caribbean and Asian groups. Incidence of illness is high and is effected by such things as dietary habit, increased smoking and increased alcohol consumption. Problems of language and cultural differences especially amongst Asian women often increase the difficulty of health and medical care delivery.

5.132 We have found that some Health Service practices are perceived by ethnic minorities to lead to less favourable treatment. Ethnic minority groups mentioned the following points which have been highlighted by the Race Relations Unit of the City Council:

(i) less resourcing of screening for and research into race/genetic-linked disease;

(ii) names in some groups, e.g. Turkish, Chinese, Indian, are different from the British pattern — this can cause delay or confusion at clinic or surgery attendances;

(iii) psychiatrists are felt to be more ready to diagnose psychosis or schizophrenia in some ethnic groups, especially in Afro-Caribbean men;

(iv) there is clear need for appropriate communication in languages other than English. We noted that information is increasingly multilingual and that interpreter services do exist in some hospitals;

(v) non-Christian faith groups are not well catered for in formal hospital arrangements for religious needs although some have attempted to make appropriate provision;

(vi) diets of Jewish, Muslim, Hindu and Rastafarian patients are influenced by religious belief. Some hospitals recognize these special needs, others are more reluctant to do so;

(vii) there has been too little attention to the training of health workers for a multi-ethnic population.

Evidence from the health service itself suggests that many of these issues are recognized and that some hospitals and General Practice surgeries are giving attention to them. The good practice of some needs to be adopted by others. Different races, cultures and languages provide challenges which the Health Service is trying to meet.

Inner City Partnership funding

5.133   The Birmingham Inner City Partnership devotes some of its
resources to health needs. First, to seek new approaches to
service provision in specific areas of high deprivation. Second,
to seek new ways of improving primary care facilities and practices.
Third, to encourage cross-sector projects (e.g. between health and
welfare, housing and education provision). Fourth, to enable the sick
elderly to remain in the community rather than go into hospital. Several
projects are in operation. In Newtown and Stockland Green there has
been improvement of community health and clinical facilities and social
workers have been attached to inner city general practices in
recognition of the high incidence of social need. Various projects are
targeted on the needs of women and children, resulting in counselling
and therapy for individuals and groups in the Central Birmingham
Health Authority, an Asian mother and baby campaign and an
interpreter to help Asian women in the West Birmingham Health
Authority. Various projects are under way to help the mentally ill and
handicapped, such as a social and recreation centre in Handsworth.
Several projects support the elderly, including East Birmingham's
geriatric liaison service, and Birmingham Crossroads Care Attendants
Scheme, run by a voluntary organization to help care for people in their
homes.

A community surgery

5.134   In the Balsall Heath/North Moseley area, where standards of
health are generally low, and where the health service needs to
be more approachable especially by Asian women, several new
initiatives have been pioneered. The Ombersley Road 'Community
Surgery', in addition to its medical practice, offers a drop-in service
catering for broader needs. Patients are given access to their medical
records and encouraged to discuss their diagnosis and treatment with
the doctor. A Nurse Practitioner Project encourages nurses to adopt a
larger role both in the practice and in community care. This has proved
popular amongst Asian women who for cultural reasons prefer to talk to
another woman.

Community care

5.135   There is a national policy of transferring the care of the elderly,
the physically and mentally handicapped and the chronic sick,

from hospitals to the community. This requires an increase in community facilities, staff and funding. Health promotion and the encouragement of healthy life styles, the proper use of screening techniques such as those for cancer of the breast, blood pressure checks and others, all require more facilities, health workers and funds. In 1985 the South Birmingham Health Authority, covering Bartley Green, Weoley, Selly Oak, Moseley, Billesley, Brandwood, Bournville, Northfield and Longbridge, introduced a new structure to improve health care. In the priority areas of the elderly, mentally ill and mentally handicapped, new strategies are being pursued. They include a commitment to provide services in a community setting rather than in an institutional environment. This implies a significant shift in the pattern of funding.

Conclusion

5.136   Our examination of the South and Central districts indicates there is a particular concentration of problems relating to deprivation in the inner city where poverty, poor housing, language problems, lack of cars and telephones all make medical and other services less accessible. Intervention tends to be on an emergency basis. It is also clear that some services outside the inner city have obvious deficiences, especially psychogeriatrics and community services for the elderly. It has to be stressed that health care is not the responsibility of the health authorities alone. The local authority, through its agencies of Environmental Services, including urban renewal, Housing Services, Social Services, Leisure and Recreation Services, is also closely involved. Voluntary organizations, the churches and other faiths, and employers also have roles to play. The five community Health Councils act in a monitoring and advocacy role. Individuals also need to accept personal primary responsibility for their own physical health; but all too frequently deprivation, in one form or another, limits choice and consequently responsibility.

(j) **Inner City Partnership Programme**

Introduction

5.137   This section describes the Inner City Partnership Programme, which is the largest single corporate activity by public bodies to address deprivation in Birmingham. The City has Inner City Partnership status under the 1978 Inner Urban Areas Act. The

Partnership has a special committee consisting of the City Council, the five Birmingham Area Health Authorities and representatives of central government departments. Resources are provided annually: in 1986/87 £26.4 million was set aside for the Birmingham Partnership. Central government provides 75 per cent of the resources for each funded project whilst the local authority or health authority has to resource the other 25 per cent. Central government has committed £25 million per year for the period 1988/89 – 1990/91. Nearly three quarters of a million people live in the Birmingham Inner City Partnership area.

Projects

5.138 Over 90 per cent of the projects in 1986/87 were under the authority of the City Council. Some 2,200 projects were funded. 38 per cent of the Partnership spending in 1986/87 was directed to economic objectives concerned with local economic regeneration. Voluntary organizations spent over £11m of the available £26.4m. Many of the projects funded by these means have been mentioned in previous sections of this chapter. The projects mainly operate in the Partnership area (see map 1.2 on page 158).

Objectives

5.139 The aims of the Partnership have become more 'specific'. Targeting is now towards projects with a visible, quantifiable effect which residents can recognize. Three key aims stand out: inner city economic regeneration; improving derelict land and buildings; and enhancing personal services with the aim of encouraging self-help. Inner city projects act as catalysts to encourage spending from the City Council's 'main programmes' and also seek to attract private sector resources. They also develop new approaches to problems and projects which would not be funded otherwise.

Policy confusion

5.140 The welcome but limited resources of the Partnership may only result in managing urban decline, rather than positive renewal. People and their problems may simply be transferred elsewhere. There are sometimes conflicts over policy direction and inner city policy control between Whitehall ministries. Inner city policy is often seen as separate, unco-ordinated initiatives by different government departments and dominated by short-term project bidding. These views are widely held by City Council departments, voluntary organizations and inner city residents. Outside some small areas within the inner city it is clear that the aggregate impact of all these programmes has not so far been equal to the needs of Urban Priority Areas.

Successes

5.141 Concentration of Inner City Partnership funding on inner city issues has had notable successes. The housing enveloping scheme was started in this way and transferred to the main housing programme; area caretakers were appointed on council housing estates and in urban renewal areas; industrial improvement areas have been developed (including an upgrading of the Jewellery Quarter); small factory units were made available; Aston Science Park was created. A significant part of the Partnership's funding has gone to voluntary organizations and increasingly has been concentrated upon the needs of ethnic minorities.

Government policy

5.142 Inner City policy has been under review by the government. 'Action for Cities' indicates changes in the Government's management of urban policy to reflect new priorities with strong reliance upon the role of the private sector in economic regeneration. The long-term role of local government is being reduced. There is now more direct central government intervention, more reliance on private sector action and the creation of further quasi state bodies e.g. Urban Development Corporations, Housing Action Trusts, to implement policy. Various ongoing ministry programmes and a few new programmes are outlined, but the new proposals, whilst welcome, do not go far enough in developing an integrated response to the problems of Urban Priority Areas.

Partnership review

5.143 The City Council's own Partnership annual review of 1987 expresses the need to work co-operatively with others, in the private and voluntary sectors. Five other matters are emphasized in the Council's review:

   (i) increase efforts for co-ordination and concentration of action on specific geographical areas;

  (ii) extend this concept of targeting to selected community-based issues such as care in the community and crime prevention;

 (iii) set clearer aims for projects and monitor their effectiveness;

 (iv) explore new ways of involving local communities in urban regeneration;

  (v) improve the image of Birmingham's inner city.

The Commission welcomes these emphases.

(k) Conclusions

5.144   The Commission draws attention to three conclusions which we believe range across the topic areas of this chapter. First, many of the issues and opportunities in Urban Priority Areas require to be tackled on an inter-agency basis, particularly at local level. Second, residents of Urban Priority Areas should wherever possible be involved in helping to influence and formulate the decisions of agencies which affect their well-being. Self-confidence and self-esteem are important for the future of such areas. Third, we recognize the changing role of many agencies, whether they be local authority departments, voluntary agencies, commercial and industrial bodies, central government agencies, the police, the health service. This provides an opportunity for agencies to re-think their approach to Urban Priority Areas because in future there will be less reliance on traditional agency approaches. A more flexible, wide-ranging, approach to service delivery is developing in parallel with a degree of withdrawal of state involvement.

PART IV

Christian Perspectives on the City

Chapter Six

CHRISTIAN PERSPECTIVES ON THE CITY

Introduction

6.1   This chapter, prepared by a group under the chairmanship of
Bishop Lesslie Newbigin, offers an interpretation, from a
particular perspective, of what is happening in a cosmopolitan,
economically divided City as it strives for unity and renewal. Inevitably
the chapter uses some of the symbolic language of the Christian faith
and different people would develop the overall perspective using
different terms and different emphases. The Christian tradition, as the
variety of Churches in Birmingham bear witness, is a varied one. That
rich variety can never be contained in one statement.

6.2   We do not claim by virtue of our corporate experience or our
Christian faith to have all the answers to the problems of the
stark divisions in our City between squalor and poverty on one
hand, and comfort and plenty on the other. We do claim to place the
struggle of our City towards justice and renewal within our particular
framework of the Christian tradition. We seek to stand with those who,
in the past in our City, have been inspired by God's action for all people
in Jesus Christ. They were impelled by their conviction to speak and act
for a vision of human society spoken of in the Bible which includes and
values all people. That vision is, for Christians, in keeping with the
fatherly and creative purpose of God for all people, as revealed through
Jesus Christ and through the Holy Spirit of God within and beyond the
Church down to our own times.

6.3   We offer this theological section to our fellow Christians and all
our fellow citizens for reflection and debate. That may demand
work with unfamiliar material. We believe it could open fresh
horizons, attitudes and approaches to developing a City and community
for all the people of Birmingham as we approach and enter the twenty-
first century.

Cities in the Christian Tradition

6.4   We have been accustomed to think of world history as the
        history of civilization, of the development of those qualities
        which make for a good city and nurture good citizens. This
owes much to the Greek vision of the city, but it has roots also in the
Bible and the Christian tradition. The city is the place where human
life, for better or for worse, is concentrated, the place to which people
come together for protection, for commerce and industry, the place
where peoples, cultures and creeds meet and mingle, where new ideas,
new arts, new skills are born and nurtured. It is the place where both
human greatness and human wickedness flourish. This double character
of the city is one of the constant themes of the Bible. The ancient story
of the Tower of Babel symbolizes the dark side of the city — the story
of human pride over-reaching itself and ending in disaster. Babel,
Babylon, is the archetypal symbol of the imperialisms that have
trampled across human history, powers which are remembered today
for their cultural achievements but which Israel experienced as brutal
tyrannies — Babylon, Nineveh, Persia, Greece and Rome. In the last
book of the Bible, the city of Rome is the great harlot, seducing,
exploiting and enslaving all the peoples of the world. But the Bible also
celebrates the city as something to be cherished. Love for the city of
Jerusalem is one of the constant themes of the prophets, and Jesus is in
their succession when he weeps over the city, pleading with Jerusalem
to acknowledge her true saviour. And finally the Bible ends with the
vision of the holy city coming down as a gift from God, the place of
supreme beauty into which all the nations will bring their treasure. The
Bible does not authorize any nostalgia for the country as against the
city. The end of the human journey, according to Scripture, is not
paradise regained — a return to Eden — but the new Jerusalem, the
city which God has prepared for us. The earliest Christian communities
were city congregations and Rome quickly became the most influential
of the Christian churches. When Rome itself, the eternal city, was
sacked by the barbarians, Augustine penned his 'City of God', giving a
vision which was to shape the history of Europe for the next thousand
years.

6.5   Our own century is witnessing an unparalleled urban explosion.
        Worldwide there are now 290 cities with more than one million
        people and in many countries more than half of the total
population lives in the capital city. People in their thousands and
millions are drawn from the countryside into the cities to find work and
to escape from the restrictions of village life into the anonymity of the
city. At the same time a reverse movement takes place: those with the

means to do so escape from the city into the neighbouring country in search of peace and quiet. The double effect of this is the increasing urbanization of the countryside and the dereliction of the inner city.

6.6   The City of Birmingham has exemplified all these world-wide trends and still does so. From its earliest days it has grown through the coming in of people in search of work — first from other parts of England, then from Ireland, Wales and Scotland, then from Europe and eventually from almost every part of the world. It has notably exemplified the virtues of the city — its crafsmanship, its entrepreneurial skills, its pioneering work in municipal government, its rich cultural tradition and its role in the political life of the nation. It also exemplifies the darker side of urban life and, very specially at this time, the problems of decay in the inner city areas and in some housing estates.

6.7   Our hope in this Report is to speak a word as Christians to all our fellow citizens — Christians and others — out of the faith which we hold. We seek to learn from the Christian tradition how to interpret for this present time God's word of warning and promise for our City.

The Church in the City

6.8   The good news which Jesus brought and which we proclaim was that 'the Kingdom of God has drawn near'. We can perhaps understand this phrase better if we use the word 'kingship'. Jesus' message was that God's kingship, his wise and loving rule over all peoples and all events, has come near. He announced its coming and himself embodied its presence and its power. That power was effective in releasing people from all kinds of oppression, physical and spiritual. He healed the sick, cleansed the lepers, fed the hungry, forgave the sinners and gave hope to the hopeless. But, in the end, his power was effective not in establishing a worldly empire but in what looked like defeat and humiliation — the cross. For most people that was the end of the story of Jesus. But for the small company of those who had been called and prepared for special responsibility as his witnesses it was disclosed — in the resurrection of Jesus and the gift of the Spirit — that what looked like defeat was in fact victory — the final victory of God against the powers that oppose God. This small community — the Church — became the bearer of the secret of the kingdom. It lives in the power of the Spirit of God, the Spirit of Jesus, who gives us in the midst of our struggle with evil the foretaste of victory.

6.9   We seek to speak together in the name of our one Lord. We know that our present separation into different ecclesial communities is contrary to our calling. We are earnestly seeking to overcome these divisions. We are thankful to God that there is a long history of co-operation among the Birmingham churches, going back to the early years of this century and now expressed in the life and work of the Birmingham Council of Christian Churches. Although we have often been guilty of seeking our own advantage and our own reputation, we know that we exist not for ourselves but for the service of God and as a sign, instrument and foretaste of his kingdom. We exist as churches not for ourselves but for the whole human community.

6.10   The Church fulfils its calling not only by preaching the kingdom but also by being itself a foretaste of the kingdom, a place where the freedom and fellowship and happiness of God's home are already enjoyed — even if only as a foretaste, a 'starter'. The business of the Church is not primarily to tell people how they ought to behave, but to invite them to share in good news about what has actually happened and is going to happen, in a secret which makes everything in life different. Sharing in that secret certainly changes behaviour, but the good news is first and the good behaviour second. Gospel comes before law. Jesus did not write a book of instructions, he shared a secret with a group of friends so that they could share it with others. It is, as Paul says, an open secret, one to be shared. But it is still a secret, a mystery — for how can one believe that a crucified man is the sovereign lord of all, that giving life away is the way to find it, that at the heart of sacrifice there is the assurance of victory?

6.11   When Jesus taught his disciples to pray for the coming of God's kingdom he taught them to interpret this as the doing of God's will 'on earth as it is done in heaven'. He gave, in teaching and example, vivid illustrations of what this doing of God's will would be like. But he did not lay down a code of laws. He did not provide a blue-print for a future society. If he had done so it would have been quickly out of date and irrelevant. Instead he formed a community and entrusted to this community, guided by the Spirit, the task of interpreting his revelation of the kingdom in new situations as they carried the good news to every nation and culture (John 16:1–15).

6.12   This community, when it is true to its nature and calling, does not exist to lay down laws or offer instructions to the rest of the world. It bears witness to the good news of the kingdom by pointing people to Jesus in whom the kingdom is present, and by embodying in its own life a foretaste of the freedom, the justice, the gladness and the fellowship of the kingdom. It has always been, and will probably always be, a small minority of the human race. Its significance in no way depends upon its size. As a sign and foretaste of the kingdom it is the bearer both of good news and of bad news. For those who are willing to follow Jesus in sharing and bearing the burden of the world's sin and wrong, it is the bearer of good news: the news that Jesus reigns and shall reign to the end and in the end. To those who decline the invitation, who are content to go along with and to profit by the world's wrong, it is the bearer of bad news: the news that the road they are travelling ends in disaster. Like the prophets of Israel, and like Jesus himself, it has both to invite and to warn: Jesus who has come as Saviour will come as Judge. The judgment is not on the basis of profession of faith but on the basis of deeds, and the judgment begins now and begins with judgment on those who belong to the household of God.

The Church in Birmingham

6.13   In Birmingham, as in almost all the other cities of the world, this community, the Church, exists and has existed from the earliest days of the City. In spite of its grievous sins and failures, it has made and continues to make a very significant contribution to the life of the City, both in its more prosperous suburban areas and in the deprived areas to which the report of the Archbishop's Commission has drawn special attention. We are concerned, as were the Archbishop's Commissioners, to strengthen the hands of the churches in the UPA's, but we would first draw attention to the strengths which are already there. We give in Chapter 4 an account of Christian action and activity. These strengths are to be found both in the 'mainline' churches which have a long history in this country, and also in the many Evangelical and Pentecostal congregations including those who embody the traditions of West Africa and the Caribbean. Many of them share to the full the multiple forms of deprivation to which the Archbishop's Commission drew attention. But in the midst of their trouble they draw strength from the biblical message. They meet week by week to remember, to rehearse, to re-enact the events of that story which Christians understand as the clue to the whole human and cosmic story. As they do so, this story becomes their own story, the way in which they understand their role in the universal story. For many, especially perhaps in the black-led churches, the great liberation stories of the Bible provide the framework through which they are helped to understand the contemporary struggle to find freedom from the powers that seem to overwhelm the poor, the unemployed, the black. 'Liberation Theology' as developed in Latin America has not been widely accepted in Britain; the Birmingham UPA is not exactly the same as the Brazilian slum. But there are enough similarities to ensure that, here too, the story of the Exodus sounds a call both for anger and for hope among those who are the victims of multiple deprivation. Those who have learned to live in the world of the Bible, to cross the Red Sea in defiance of Pharaoh's army, to return with singing from exile to Babylon and to witness the resurrection of the crucified Jesus, do not feel defeated. They have the assurance of victory in the midst of trouble, and that enables them to go on acting with hope.

6.14   This capacity to go on acting hopefully in apparently hopeless situations is perhaps the greatest contribution that the Church can bring to the well-being of the city. It is true that this kind of faith, grounded in the biblical story of redemption, has sometimes been converted into an escapist piety, an invitation to turn one's back on the troubles of the city and to look for consolation in another world. The ultimate hope offered by the gospel is indeed one that reaches beyond death — our own personal death and the final dissolution of the cosmic order. But what is promised and pledged in the gospel is hope for the world, not just hope for the individual soul. It is hope for the coming of the City of God. The privatization of hope is a distortion of the gospel. Resolute and sustained action in the face of disappointment can only be sustained by shared confidence in a worthwhile future. This kind of confidence is in short supply today. It is part of the secret of the kingdom that hope shines most brightly in the midst of trouble, that the body which bears the marks of Jesus' passion shares the power of his resurrection. There is, perhaps, a gift here which the more comfortable churches may receive from churches which seem to need more help. The suburb and the inner city need each other.

Sinned Against and Sinning

6.15   The ministry of Jesus is depicted in the gospels as a mighty battle with the power of the enemy of God, the power that enslaves and dehumanizes the children of God. Those who minister the Gospel in UPAs, as elsewhere, know that the 'enemy', the 'oppressor', is not to be identified with any human person or agency. The ultimate enemy is not any human person or agency but that power which is the source of sin and death. The redemption wrought by Jesus was first of all deliverance from the power of sin. The gospel has to address both the sinner and the one who is sinned against. In fact all of us are both. It has often been and still is easy for those who are in comfortable circumstances to blame the poverty, sickness and misery of others (secretly if not openly) on their sins. To say that the poor and the sick are so because of their own fault is one of the forms of deceit by which the comfortable seek to protect themselves. In understandable revolt against this lie, many Christians have followed secular analysts in affirming that poverty, sickness, illiteracy and other forms of diminishment are the fault of other people, of the rich, of the social and economic order, of 'the system'. They divide human society into two classes: oppressors and oppressed. Jesus, they affirm, was on the side of the oppressed, and that is where the Church must be.

6.16   This is an understandable protest against a comforting lie, but it is not the whole truth. It is profoundly demeaning to the 'oppressed' to suggest that they have no personal responsibility for the total situation of which their suffering is a part. Any honest description of the break-down of human well-being in our cities must be in terms which are both personal and structural. The break-down of family life, the sexual promiscuity which so often produces it, the wholesale delivery of pornography and violence into the living rooms where parents and children pass their time, the massive increase in the practice of abortion, the failure of parents to discipline their children — all of these are the fruit of a philosophy which accepts self-seeking as the norm of human conduct and pleasure as the goal of human living. This is in turn fuelled by powerful interests which depend upon the multiplication of new wants among those whose basic material needs are already met. This complex web of evil cannot be understood in terms of personal sin alone nor in terms of systemic evil alone. Both are involved. There are commercial, social and economic structures which embody evil forces and which make it easier to sin than not to sin. But individual persons are responsible for consenting or resisting.

6.17   The sickness of our inner cities is part of the sickness of our whole society, and the healing ministry of the Church is rendered ineffective when there is no clear understanding of the source of the disease. It is misleading to set personal responsibility and systemic evil over against one another. It is wrong to suggest that solutions are to be found simply by 'changing the system', and it is also wrong to suggest that the solution lies entirely in personal conversion. Both are involved, for true conversation has systemic implications. We are responsible persons within a network of relationships which together constitute 'the system'. The call to follow Jesus is indeed a call to conversion, to a radical change of direction for one's whole life. But true conversion will involve not only the direction of one's personal relationships but also the direction of one's public, civic, political and cultural activities. It is society as a whole, the rich and the poor, who are called to radical conversion. And the teaching of Jesus consistently suggests that it is the rich who are in the greatest need of a radical change of direction.

The Church as Sign of the Kingdom

6.18   We have said that the Church is called to be (in Birmingham as everywhere) sign, instrument and foretaste of the kingdom.
Before going on to suggest how this calling is to be fulfilled it is necessary to guard the statement against misunderstanding. God is king over all creation and it would be a monstrous absurdity to suggest that his kingdom is domesticated within the Church. He is Lord of all, all people are made in his image and the evidences of that fact are — thank God — visible among people of every kind, of every creed, of every culture. The light of God, present in full splendour in Jesus, shines on every human being and it is reflected wherever people respond to God in loving response to the needs of others. The light does indeed shine in darkness: there is much that tries to quench it. But it cannot be quenched and its beams extend to every corner of God's creation. Therefore those who have acknowledged that light in Jesus will welcome, cherish and rejoice in every reflection of that light wherever it is seen. And this, of course, is not a matter of 'religion' but of everything that reflects however faintly the love of God. Moreover the Church, called to be a sign of the kingdom, is and has always been guilty of acting in an exactly contrary manner, of obscuring the light, of denying the truth. That has always been so. The same Peter who was chosen to be the rock on whom Christ would build his Church was — in almost the same breath — called an agent of Satan. And that terrible charge was made because Peter was not willing to accept that the way of God's kingly rule is the way of the cross. Whenever the Church tries to avoid that costly way, it falls under judgment.

6.19   However this does not countermand the calling of the Church.
It is essential to say this, because all kinds of movements have been hailed throughout history as signs of the kingdom and have become in the end agencies of disaster. The fundamental fact is that the kingly rule of God has been decisively manifested and put into effect in the cross and resurrection of Jesus, and the community which confesses that remains (in spite of its sins) the body to which, and to which alone, the specific calling is addressed — to be sign, instrument

and foretaste of the kingdom, the kingdom which is for all. It is by that calling that the Church will be judged.
How may the Church be an authentic sign of the kingdom?

A Community of Praise

6.20 The Church's first privilege and duty is to be a community of praise. It is important to begin with this, perhaps just because it is so offensive to a society dominated by technology and oriented towards 'practical solutions' to our urgent 'problems'. If we begin (as our culture teaches us to do) by defining a set of problems and looking for solutions, then the Church's worship will appear the most irrelevant of exercises. But (and this can not be said too often) the Christian life begins from another point. It begins with a radical 'U-turn' a turning round which causes us to discover that amazing grace is the real thing we have to deal with, a goodness so amazing and overwhelming that our first response can only be adoring praise. The Church was born in an explosion of joy when the first disciples knew that death and sin had been swallowed up in victory. The life of the Church is authentic when it is the continuing fall-out from that explosion — a kind of radioactivity which is not lethal but liberating and renewing. This is not escapism. In a world tormented by 'problems' and driven by anxieties (including the anxiety to justify ourselves to our own consciences) the setting aside of time and place for praising, celebrating, enjoying and giving thanks for the boundless goodness of God is the first privilege of the Church and the first condition for its being a sign of the kingdom. From this praise, when it is authentic, actions flow which make it possible for people to believe that, in spite of the appalling evils of the world, God does reign. It is the crucified Jesus who was raised from death, and it is when the Church bears in its life the scars of the continuing battle with the powers of evil that it can rejoice in that victory. Like the precious ointment poured out on the feet of Jesus by a forgiven sinner, the actions of the Church which are authentic signs of the kingdom will be the spontaneous acts of loving and caring which are the overflow from a thankful heart.

A Community of Responsibility

6.21 The Church is called to be a community in which people learn to live in mutual responsibility to and with their neighbours.
Traditional rural societies, where people live in small close-knit communities, know well that human life depends upon the

acceptance of mutual responsibility. In the anonymity of city life this mutual dependence is less obvious. In the city, the individual is easily seduced into an individualism which supposes that happiness and fulfilment come from being able to pursue one's own interests and desires. But this is an illusion. Urbanization does not alter the fundamentals of human nature. The truth is that human beings find happiness and fulfilment in a life of mutual caring and mutual accountability. The terrible damage which unemployment does to the human person is not the loss of income but the loss of this bonding in a network of mutual responsibility. It thus drives its victims into themselves. This is why the problems of the UPAs cannot be met except by programmes which enlist the personal commitment of their people in shared action for the community. The Christian congregation, living in the light and power of the biblical story, is called to be and often is a place where ordinary people, even deeply hurt and humiliated people, discover their true humanity in serving one another and their neighbours for Jesus' sake. In a society which speaks much of 'rights' but little of the duties without which all claims to rights are illusion, the Church acknowledges that the debt we owe to Christ outweighs any claim we could make for our rights, and that the attorney appointed by Christ to receive discharge of the debt is our neighbour — whoever that may be. No welfare state is viable unless it contains enough people who put responsibilities before rights; and the Church, as the community of praise, is a proper place for the nurturing of such people. Here is where we must look for the fruits of a genuine conversion to Christ and his kingdom. It creates people who accept responsibility for others, who accept the risks and responsibilities of leadership in the community. It nurtures a sense of civic responsibility. It produces (for example) people who (following St. Paul) see the payment of their rates and taxes not as an infringement of personal freedom but as the acknowledgement of a debt they owe and an expression of their commitment to the welfare of city and nation. This commitment will be expressed primarily in the way that Christians discharge their responsibilities in their various secular callings, and also through their participation in political and voluntary service of all kinds to the community of city, nation and world. It is in these secular tasks that 'the priesthood of all believers' is to find its primary exercise.

A Community of Reconciliation

6.22   The divisions which tear society apart and which marginalize many of the people of the inner cities are as much cultural as economic. The Church is a society which can, and in some measure does, bridge these divisions. Congregations do not find this easy. To remain content with a fellowship which embraces only people of the same education, race or class is a failure to rise to the full meaning of churchmanship. Full and free fellowship in a congregation which includes people of very different kinds is never an easy achievement. It may, and often does, entail tension and conflict. To achieve it requires patience and perseverance. But there are many congregations where the members rejoice in the enrichment brought to their lives by sharing a common life in Christ with people of vastly different education, culture and style of life. Such congregations are signs of hope for the whole community.

A Community of Witness

6.23   As sign and foretaste of the Kingdom of God, the Church is called to bear witness to that kingship as the reality with which every person and every institution must in the end reckon. This witness embraces both the two activities which are designated (and often falsely opposed to each other) as evangelism and social action. The Church has to be involved in both. Preaching which is not authenticated by actions that illustrate the rule of God, will be empty words; social and political action which fails to point beyond itself to Jesus as the one in whom the kingly rule of God is actually embodied will betray people with false hopes, for no social order can provide that which will satisfy the deepest longings of the human heart. So word and deed must go together. And because 'judgement begins at the house of God' the Church must resolutely face those areas of her life where practice contradicts message. Churches which are unable to achieve reconciliation among themselves are not well placed to preach peace to others.

6.24   This two-fold prophetic ministry has to be exercised both in the immediate neighbourhood and in the wider life of the city and nation. In the first place, each local community of Christians needs to engage in a sustained attempt to relate the faith to the concrete realities of life in the neighbourhood. Reflection in the light of Christian faith and appropriate action will form a pattern which is constantly repeated as action leads on to further reflection and so to renewed action. The Archbishop's Commission has suggested ways in which the local church may be helped to engage in this kind of reflection and action ('Faith in the City' Appendix A). We set our views out in Chapters 4 and 7. The Anglican Diocese of Birmingham has developed its own scheme for this purpose (see Chapter 4).

6.25   In the second place the Church is called to a prophetic ministry in relation to the wider communities of City and Nation. The Church bears witness to that reality by which all peoples and all policies will finally be judged, namely the kingly rule of God as manifest in Jesus. This does not mean, however, that the Church is authorized to issue advice to the agencies which have responsibility for the ordering of public life. According to St. Paul, the civic authority has its own mandate from God, even when (as was the case under the Roman Empire) the source of the mandate is not recognized. The Church is required to acknowledge the separate and distinct authority of the State, although it is also required to remind those who hold office in the State that they are responsible to God who is the author of their mandate.

6.26   In an analogous way the Church has to recognize the proper autonomy of the various areas of human knowledge. Sciences such as economics have their proper autonomy and this has to be respected. Theology cannot replace economics, nor can theologians take over the responsibilities of economists. But this autonomy is relative, not absolute. All sciences depend upon initial assumptions which cannot be validated from within the science in question. Economics, for example, depends upon assumptions about the ways in which human beings can be expected to behave, and about what human beings want and need. All of these assumptions are open to examination from the point of view of theology. While avoiding the temptation to transgress the proper boundaries of the various secular disciplines, the Church is nevertheless under obligation to remind all involved of that ultimate reality by which all things human will be finally judged.

A Community among other Communities

6.27   We have been speaking of the Church as sign, instrument and foretaste of the kingdom of God. But we cannot forget that the membership of all the Christian churches put together makes up only a small minority of the population of the City. And God's purpose, God's caring, God's love is for the whole city. God calls some to be his witnesses for all, but that in no way means that those whom he calls have a monopoly of his love. To suppose that God has a special care for Christians is to misunderstand the gospel at its heart. The majority of our fellow citizens do not believe what we believe. Many of them have residual allegiances to some form of Christianity but it is no longer their controlling belief. Many are adherents — more or less faithful — of one or other of the great world religions. Their presence has raised new questions in the minds of the native Christians. We have been accustomed to the fact that large numbers of our fellow citizens have abandoned all living religious belief and practice. We have acknowledged a responsibility (in theory if not in vigorous practice) to bring the gospel to them building on their residual allegiance. But we have not been accustomed to thinking about the relation of our faith to that of our devout Muslim, Hindu and Sikh neighbours. Many of them are plainly more godly than the majority of the native citizens. In many cases they are seeking to preserve traditions of family life and discipline which the nominally Christian majority has lost. What place should they have in a Christian vision for the City? These questions raise very large issues which cannot be adequately probed in a short report, but we suggest four guiding principles.

6.28   The first is that Christians should wholeheartedly welcome and rejoice in the evidences of the work of God's grace in the lives of people of other faiths and people of no religious faith. It is fundamental to our faith that God has made all people in his image, fashioned to respond to his love; that Jesus is the light shining on every human being so that reflections of that light are to be found everywhere; and that the reflections of this light are not only in what we call 'religion' but in everything that mirrors even a glint of the goodness and grace of God. The goodness of the non-religious is often a form of God's judgement upon the religious: it was not the godly priest or Levite, but the semi-pagan Samaritan who reflected the grace of God in Jesus' story of the 'good Samaritan'. It is indeed true that in the light of Christ all human beings are sinners, but it is not our business to ferret out the sins of our non-Christian neighbours. It is Christ who is judge, and the judgment is only the dark shadow thrown by the light. Our business, as fellow-sinners, is to recognize and rejoice in the light that enlightens every person of whatever faith or no-faith.

6.29   Secondly it follows that we must seek out and develop those areas of our civic life in which people of all faiths can co-operate for the common good. This is especially relevant in the UPAs where many of the people of Muslim, Hindu and Sikh faith are living. There is need for the churches to initiate friendly contacts with the representatives of the other faith-communities to explore ways in which they can work together to restore hope and to stimulate co-operative enterprize in the deprived areas of the City. There is much here in which differences of religious faith need be no barrier to collaboration.

6.30   Thirdly, the local congregation must be a place where people of all faiths can find a welcome. The good news of which we are the bearers is for all. It would be an intolerable sort of racism to suggest that the gospel is only for people of a certain ethnic origin. It is for all, and we must learn the ways of sharing it lovingly and sensitively with people of all faiths in our City. Formal inter-faith dialogue is an exercise for those with expert knowledge of the different faith–traditions, but we can all be involved in normal neighbourly conversation — and this should include all our neighbours and should provide the opportunities to learn of the religious experience of our neighbours, to share our faith and to communicate the invitation of a caring congregation. We shall usually find that our Muslim and Sikh neighbours are equally willing to talk about their faith and to invite us to their gatherings. We have much to learn which may cause us to re-think our own assumptions and commitments. But we are entrusted with a unique treasure which is not our own — namely the good news that the sovereign lord of all creation has acted in infinite love and humility to deliver all humankind from the power of sin and death and to open for us the gate of life. That news we cannot keep to ourselves.

6.31 Fourthly, we must be concerned about what is being taught in the schools. Education is, in an important respect, concerned with carrying forward into the future the good traditions of the past which have shaped our society. These traditions have been grounded in the Christian faith, and — until recently — Religious Education in schools was concerned with teaching the essentials of the Christian faith. Today, responding to the multi-faith character of the City, RE is much and rightly concerned with enabling children to understand other world faiths. It seems certain, however, that what chiefly shapes the understanding of children is not what is taught in 'RE', but what is taught in the rest of the curriculum. Insofar as this teaches children to believe that the world can be satisfactorily understood without reference to any ultimate religious belief, it is the occasion for profound anxiety among many (chiefly Muslim) people of other faiths. They respond by insisting on thorough religious teaching outside of school hours. The Christian churches have not, in general, matched this effort. The present danger is that the ultimate effect of the school-experience for most children will be to lead them to conclude that religious faith — Christian or otherwise — is an optional but not an essential part of understanding the world. No issue could be more vital for the future of our society than this question of the role of religious teaching in the schools, and the presence of the other faith communities in Birmingham is challenging us to look at this in a new light. For this we may be thankful.

Ministerial Leadership in the Christian Community

6.32   As in any human community, much of the effectiveness of the
Christian congregation will depend upon the leadership. Many
of our churches are heavily dependent, perhaps too much
dependent, upon the leadership of ministers trained and ordained for
full-time service. The Archbishop's Commission expressed much
concern about the character of this training and its effects upon the
ministerial leadership of UPA congregations. It made the startling
statement that present patterns of training were not merely inappropriate but positively disabling for ministry in UPAs ('Faith in the City'
6.56). The criticism made is that the normal methods of training are
'too academic' and that theology is seen as 'a deductive science' in
which 'Christian truth is conceived as a system derived from divine
revelation and human reason, and growth in understanding is aided by
historical and philosophical disciplines (*op. cit.* 3.30). There are issues
raised here which urgently need more careful examination. If Christian
theology cannot be merely 'deductive' in the sense of a series of logical
deductions from verbal propositions believed to be divinely revealed, it
certainly cannot be merely 'inductive' — the result of reflection on our
situation. Authentic Christian theology derives from God's revelation of
himself in Christ, and must involve the disciplined use of human reason
in seeking to grasp that revelation, to respond to it, and to relate it to
contemporary issues. Nor can Christian theology decline the task of
exploring the bearing of that revelation upon what is learned in the
academic disciplines of history, philosophy and natural science. The
crucial question is whether the biblical testimony to revelation is looked
at from outside, in the framework of another way of understanding the
world (for example the modern scientific world–view, or Marxism, or
the Vedanta) or whether one is looking at it from the inside, as one who
lives in the biblical story and accepts it as the framework within which
one tries to understand the world. One of the disabling factors in the
church's contemporary witness is the split between those who accept a
'historical–critical' approach to the Scripture and those who reject it.
The great strength of the Black-led and other churches referred to in
para. 6.13 above derives in part from the fact that they feel able to live
in the world of the Bible, to accept its story as their story and so to
understand and deal with contemporary events with the Bible as their
mental framework. On the other hand, a type of scholarship which
treats the scriptures merely as an object for critical examination by a
detached and uncommitted scholar is unlikely to provide resources for
the Christian warfare in the inner city or anywhere else.

6.33   But the ministerial leadership of the churches is not confined to the full-time ordained ministry. There is a great deal of ministerial leadership given by lay people who are prepared for and trained in it through many formal and informal arrangements. This is true of many of the more vigorous congregations in the UPAs. Birmingham has rich resources for the training of leadership for the churches, both in the University of Birmingham, the colleges of education, the theological colleges and Bible schools and also many more informal programmes of Christian education. Birmingham is well equipped to respond to the penetrating challenge raised by 'Faith in the City' in regard to ministerial training.

Affirmations for Public Policy

6.34   We have been speaking of the Church as sign, instrument and foretaste of God's kingdom. We have talked of the Church because it is the community which Christ launched into the world to bear his name and continue his work. But the Church betrays its commission if it is chiefly concerned about its own growth and wellbeing. The Church's role is that of servant — a servant of God for the sake of his world. How is this service to be accomplished on behalf of a city such as Birmingham? We have affirmed that the first responsibility of the Church is to be itself faithful to its own Gospel and thus to be a place where there is already a foretaste of God's Kingdom of love, freedom and justice. In so far as the Church fails to be this it forfeits any right to speak to others. But if it is fulfilling this primary calling, what can it say to those who have responsibility for the government, industry, commerce and culture of the City? It is notoriously difficult for the Church to speak on public issues without either lapsing into platitudes or else claiming transcendent authority for positions which are by no means impregnable. Recognizing these risks, we venture to suggest five affirmations which, if accepted, would have far-reaching practical consequences.

Wellbeing and Wealth

6.35   Jesus said that a man's life does not consist in the abundance of his possessions. The one who thought otherwise is called a fool. Human experience amply bears this out. Human being does indeed require material support — food, clothing, shelter. These things have to be produced in sufficient quantity. Classical economics was concerned with marginal values in a world of shortages. Paradoxically our present economic problems in the 'developed' world are largely concerned with surpluses — surplus production of food and many other commodities, and surplus labour. Yet the world as a whole is in short supply of the essentials for living. Our economic problems cannot be solved except on a world scale; we have to learn as a human family both to produce and to share. But we shall not solve them unless we learn that human well-being is not to be measured simply by the abundance of possessions. Gross National Product is not a reliable index of human well-being. This has obvious implications for the balance between private enterprize and public spending and between manufacturing and the service industries. Both have to be evaluated in terms of human well-being. We know, to our bitter cost, that where wealth accumulates, men and women may decay.

Wellbeing and Community

6.36   It is an illusion of our culture that fulfilment and happiness can be reached by maximising the opportunities for the individual to make individual choices. There are indeed many whose range of choice is severely limited and for whom a wider range of opportunity ought to be available. But it is an illusion to imagine that happiness comes from unlimited freedom 'to have what I want and to do what I like'. Human fulfilment comes through being related to others in bonds of love, faithfulness and mutual trust. At the heart of the Christian faith is the doctrine of the Trinity — that the glory of God is not that of a solitary potentate, but the glory of love forever poured out and forever shared. According to the Scripture both creation and redemption are an expression of that divine love, and God is ceaselessly seeking to bind us to himself in bonds of faithful love to him and to one another. If this is the reality with which we have ultimately to reckon, as Christians believe that it is, then it follows that human fulfilment and happiness are achieved, or approximated, when human beings are brought into relationships in which they are responsible to one another and help one another. It is widely recognized today that a disastrous mistake in public policy was made when, in the name of 'amenity', streets of terraced houses were demolished and replaced by high-rise blocks of flats. The poverty and deprivation of the former condition was replaced by greater 'amenity', but attention was not given to creating neighbourhoods for an inter-dependent community, arguably the prime amenity.

Community, Trust and Truth

6.37   Human community breaks down where there is no trust, and trust is created only by speaking truth. The New Testament speaks of the coming of Jesus as the coming of light 'in whom is no darkness at all', and affirms that it is when we walk in the light that we have fellowship. In one of his most drastic warnings against the inflation of verbal currency Jesus said: 'Let what you say be simply "Yes" or "No", anything more than that comes from evil.' Yet one of the most striking elements in the contemporary human situation is the 'communications explosion'. Modern technology has vastly increased the possibilities for communication information, ideas and images; it has correspondingly increased the possibilities for misinformation. Widespread cynicism about whether the words of public figures can be trusted is a deeply disturbing fact about our society. No human community can enjoy well-being where the means of communication are no longer trusted. The Church needs a vigilant concern for truthfulness, first in its own life and then in the life of city and nation.

The Recognition of Limits

6.38   Any account of contemporary society must also recognize what may be called the explosion of expectations. It it taken for granted that human beings in a 'developed' society have the right — as a matter of course — to expect a continually rising 'standard of living'. This is pure illusion having no basis in reality. We have been reminded in recent years of the fact that there are limits to growth, that the resources of our planet are not infinite, and that if the entire population of the world should even approach the standard of living now normal in the 'developed' world, the human race would face disaster. But, even setting aside the doomsday scenario of the ecologists, we have to recognize that the pursuit of this illusion is the prime cause for the persistence of poverty in a rich society. This is so for two reasons. Firstly, poverty in our society is not the absolute poverty of destitution and starvation — except for a very few. As compared with the majority of the world's poor, the people of our UPAs are well off. Their poverty is not (with some exceptions) the absence of basic biological necessities. It is the relative deprivation which separates them from the majority in society. But this relative deprivation is continuously aggravated as the spiral of demand continues to rise. To put it in another way, what were once luxuries for the few become necessities for all, and to be deprived of them is to be poor. Secondly, the demand for a higher 'standard of living' among those who have the means to satisfy their desires deflects productive resources from the provision of the basic needs of all — housing, drainage, schools and hospitals. The Church's witness to the truth, to the reality with which all human beings have in the end to reckon, must involve exposing the futile illusion that human well-being is a matter of the unlimited expansion of the power to satisfy every conceivable want, and to affirm the truth that human life achieves its true stature in the acceptance of the limits which reality imposes; that happiness does not come from the satisfaction of our wants but from the knowledge that God's family of mankind, all our fellow citizens, have access to the support of their needs.

An Indestructible Hope

6.39 Human well-being is not possible without hope. We cannot live full and happy lives with nothing to look forward to. The hope of 'progress' which sustained our Victorian forefathers in the days when Birmingham led the world in the achievement of commerce, industry and good municipal government no longer sustains us. The gospel of the resurrection of the crucified Saviour provides grounds on which it is always possible and fitting to have hope. There is little hope in evidence about the future of our society. There is indeed (and not least in the UPAs) a considerable element of nostalgia. The past is perceived as a time free from the trauma and tensions of the present. Whether this perception is true or not is not, for the moment, the issue. Human beings have always been tempted by nostalgia — from the days when the escaping Israelites in the desert began thinking of the food they had enjoyed in Egypt. But God leads his people forward. The future is always unknown and therefore always potentially frightening. Our time is no exception. But to be afraid of the future is to choose death. The faith which springs from the resurrection of the crucified Jesus gives birth to a confident hope which no disappointment can destroy. Birmingham has a great past, but that past cannot be re-created. The future will be different. It will be shaped by the radically new technologies which are already transforming industry, commerce, communications and every aspect of our common life. But the ultimate future belongs to Christ and his kingly rule, and therefore all our development and use of these new powers must be shaped by the knowledge that in the end we shall be judged by that rule, by whether or not our use of these powers has served the needs of the least of the brothers and sisters of the King (Matthew 25.31–46). That judgment is the ultimate horizon for all our activity whether in the Church or in the public life of the City. It must determine the direction of everything we attempt now. We offer this statement and affirmation in the hope that it will be found helpful by Christians and those of other faiths in Birmingham and elsewhere.

PART V

Conclusions and Recommendations

7. Conclusions and Recommendations

Chapter Seven

CONCLUSIONS AND RECOMMENDATIONS

General Themes

7.1   Later in this chapter we offer our general conclusions together
with our particular recommendations to agencies whose tasks
are concerned with particular aspects of Birmingham's life.
Many of these matters inter-connect but are separated here for ease of
treatment. First, however, we present four themes which we have
identified as woven into nearly all aspects of life in the Urban Priority
Areas and beyond.

(a) *Inter-Agency Collaboration*

7.2   Collaboration between agencies is increasing across the divides
between the public, private, voluntary and church sectors.
Chapter 5 identifies many examples, ranging from the local
Council's co-operation with the Chamber of Industry and Commerce to
create the East Birmingham Urban Development Agency, through job
creation schemes funded by MSC and run by a variety of agencies, to
intensive housing estate management schemes. Collaboration over-
comes confusion and duplication and also enables limited, scarce
funding from statutory, private and voluntary sources to be more
effectively combined and targeted.

7.3   WE URGE that all agencies, in their planning, action and
funding, should continue to develop and refine their collaboration in Urban Priority Areas.

(b) *Community Involvement*

7.4   This matter is closely related to inter-agency collaboration.
Developments which meet the real needs of people in Urban

Priority Areas can best take place when those people are involved in formulating plans and in seeing they are carried out. Some people with whom we have spoken feel alienated from decisions of local government; others feel successfully involved. Some Local Authority officers have a strong commitment to this open style of operation. Area sub-committees, neighbourhood offices, Police Consultative Committees, school governing bodies are all bodies which can help community involvement.

7.5   WE STRONGLY IDENTIFY ourselves with those who are seeking ways to improve further the involvement of local people in the processes of consultation and decision making about environmental, community and service development in their areas and about the longer term running of such programmes.

(c) *Public Expenditure*

7.6   Public sector programmes have been criticized for being over-lavish, wasteful and imperfectly targeted. We are sure there are examples where this has been so. But such criticism does not deflect us from the view that if the disadvantaged are to be helped in material ways then strongly funded public welfare programmes will be necessary. THE COMMISSION BELIEVES that public expenditure continues to be essential to the development and sustaining of social policy in housing, health care, education, community care, policing and assistance to the poor and unemployed. Private finance is drawn to well-located industrial, residential and commercial sites: it is not attracted to the deprived and the poor, whose need is greatest. Government restrictions on Local Authority expenditure make forward planning by the Local Authority difficult. The cut-back, termination or delay in programmes creates frustration, anger and falling morale among Urban Priority Area residents and those who serve them as councillors and officials. WE ARE CONCERNED at the implications of current proposals for the introduction of a Community Charge (or Poll Tax) to replace domestic rates. We must also draw attention to the greater burden which will fall on low income households if the present proposals are adopted.

(d) *Race Relations*

7.7   Good race relations are crucial to the unity of a city of one million people, 20 per cent of whom are from New Commonwealth and Pakistani cultures. That percentage is much higher in inner city Urban Priority Areas. Because of the universality of these issues, race relations have a place in virtually each section of our report. They have not been treated as a separate matter. The Commission is encouraged at the range of positive action which is being taken by many bodies to address the issues of equal opportunities and institutional racism. We are also deeply convinced that racism is still prevalent throughout our City in both overt and subtle ways.

7.8   WE URGE the continued development of positive initiatives to enable groups and individuals to become aware of racism and to adopt policies, training and appropriate monitoring to develop a City of equal opportunities.

Good Practice — Good News

7.9   Chapter 5 has described many positive and successful initiatives which serve the needs of people in Urban Priority Areas and which collaborate successfully with them. There is commitment to these tasks by a range of people from policemen to politicians, from council employees to church and voluntary workers. Good news must not be stifled by bad news. Those who speak on behalf of the disadvantaged, including the churches, should bear this in mind.

7.10   WE URGE THAT examples of good practice should be well publicised in order to give encouragement and hope to those who are committed to improving the quality of life in Urban Priority Areas, and also to suggest possible lines of action to those in similar circumstances.

Central Government

7.11   We have, in a number of places in Chapter 5, commented upon the role of central government. That is not our prime focus in this report about Birmingham. Yet we are aware of the pervading influence of policies and actions of central government affecting, as they do, the quality of life in Urban Priority Areas. Here we make only a few general comments about central government's role.

7.12   Central government has set itself a similar agenda to ours in identifying Urban Priority Areas in the inner city and elsewhere as a priority for action. We welcome the initiatives

included in 'Action for Cities'. WE URGE central government to give
continuous attention to those who are deprived and live in the inner city
and other Urban Priority Areas, by providing adequate resourcing and
by encouraging other agencies and local residents to play an active part
in the regeneration of the environment and in improving the quality of
life of such people.

7.13   We recognize that a key function of central government is that
         of controlling public finance and determining priorities for
         public expenditure. There is no real alternative to public
expenditure as the cornerstone of much, though not all, of the action
needed in the inner city and in other Urban Priority Areas. WE URGE
central government to continue to recognize the key role of public
expenditure to assist those living in such areas. Given the government's
commitment to the inner cities and other Urban Priority Areas we
would expect to see increased public expenditure to match that
commitment in order to have the sustained impact that is necessary.

7.14   The Commission points out that the mechanisms by which
         programmes are delivered to the inner city and Urban Priority
         Areas are now changing. Different agencies and different
sectors will have important changed roles to play. All these agencies
need to be committed to improving the quality of life in Urban Priority
Areas — and doing so in partnership with others.

The Christian Churches

7.15   Chapter 4 has given some account of the life of the churches in
         Birmingham in response to the circumstances of Urban
         Priority Areas. We present that account as an indication of
'good practice' for the churches. We hope that all Christian congregations in Birmingham will give time to discussion, thought and prayer
about their developing response. It is essential that that response is
thought through locally. A particular area of consideration might be a
re-assessment of the balance and relationship between concern for the
life and worship of the congregation and concern for the needs of the
wider community, and between service and evangelism. We recognize
that many Anglican churches have already begun the process through
their response to 'Faith in the City', co-ordinated originally by the
Diocese's Monitoring Group. There is also action by most other
denominations.

7.16   WE URGE that representatives of churches co-operate with other local agencies and groupings — such as area sub-committees — in contributing to the task of developing the life of the whole community. Congregations might also study the policy areas identified in chapter 5 as a basis for considering possible local response, which may be assisted by a consideration of chapter 4. Daily work, public, professional, political life are an essential part of the Church's mission and task. WE URGE all Christians to recognize it as such. These commitments can demand training. WE ENCOURAGE the plans of departments of the Church of England Diocese and of Westhill College, in the Selly Oak Colleges, in this field of training for Urban Priority Area ministry.

7.17 WE RECOGNIZE the contribution made at City-wide level by the Birmingham Council of Christian Churches, the Churches Industrial Group (Birmingham) and many specialist Christian organizations including: St. Basil's Centre, Pilgrim Social Action, the United Evangelical Project and Housing Associations. We feel that this work could be further developed at City-wide level and that support should be given to strengthening local initiatives in order to bring together local congregations/ministers/fraternals/councils of churches with community groups, other living faiths and City agencies including Area Sub-Committees and Neighbourhood Offices.

7.18 WE RECOMMEND that congregations which have not already done so take action to review the nature of the community in which they are set and possible co-operation with other congregations, as a basis for future worship, evangelism and service. (The Anglican Diocese can make available both information about its parishes and also details of the assessment methods by which the information was collected.)

7.19 WE RECOMMEND that congregations study our Chapter 6, 'Christian Perspectives', as a contribution to theological thinking about Church and City.

7.20 WE RECOMMEND that the three Presidents of the Birmingham Council of Christian Churches meet along with other church leaders and other appropriate representatives from member and non-member churches, denominations with the following aims:

   (i) to consider what further co-ordination of central action by denominations is desirable and possible;
   (ii) to consider the strengthening of the City-wide links that exist between the churches/ecumenical bodies and other agencies

(notably the City Council and the police as well as the voluntary and private sectors) in order to address the issues of Urban Priority Areas more fully.

Private Sector

7.21 The private sector plays the dominant part in the industrial and commercial life of the City. Many central government initiatives are designed to encourage wider participation by the private sector through the contracting out of local authority services, through the use of limited public funds to attract larger sums of private sector money and through the encouragement of the private sector to play a lead role in the rejuvenation of inner city areas and inner city economies. Amongst some groups in the private sector the Commission has found commitment to the renewal of the inner areas of Birmingham, a growing desire to work together with the local authority and with central government, and an increasing willingness of the private sector to assist weaker, newer ventures through advice, assistance and links with medium and larger firms.

7.22 WE ENCOURAGE the creation of 'compacts' between local industry and schools (see para. 5.68).

7.23 WE RECOMMEND that the difficulties of obtaining business insurance in Urban Priority Areas should be addressed as a matter of urgency by the Chamber of Commerce and the CBI.

7.24 WE RECOMMEND that local employers should, whenever possible, employ local labour from Urban Priority Areas and that the Public Employment Service should first ensure that there are no suitable people in the local Urban Priority Area before filling a job from outside the area.

7.25 WE RECOMMEND that job training and skills development opportunities for people in Urban Priority Areas should be reviewed by the Training Commission, local authority and employers in order to ensure adequate access by all residents of these areas to relevant training to suit their circumstances.

7.26 WE RECOMMEND that, given the changing patterns of job location, the local authority and the West Midlands Passenger Transport Authority ensure that adequate transport is available from Urban Priority Areas to areas of job expansion.

7.27   WE ENCOURAGE the development of contacts, partnership and
co-operation between voluntary and community associations
and the private sector aiming at the regeneration of local
business and residential communities.

Local Government

7.28   Local government plays a prime role in dealing with many of
the matters which are identified in this report. Its resources are
restricted. It is important to stress that Birmingham has a
proud tradition of local government. We found much dedication and
commitment amongst local politicians and local government officials.
We also found much frustration, especially over the lack of resources to
make real progress with a number of problems that were identified. The
Commission is aware of the changes affecting local government,
including budget reductions, pressures for consumer-oriented services,
and changing economic pressures in the City. We recognize the
difficulties with which the City Council is faced in making its impact.
THE COMMISSION AFFIRMS its strong belief in the important role of local
government in the City of Birmingham as it responds to new
circumstances.

Inner City Partnership Programme

7.29   This programme, which consists of nearly 3 per cent of the
total City budget, has improved parts of the inner city. It has
played an important role in assisting the voluntary sector, but
time-expired schemes create problems. We welcome and encourage the
City Council's often imaginative development of inner city projects of
its own and with other agencies. Our visits indicated the significance
many of the projects held for local people. WE RECOGNIZE AND FIRMLY
ENDORSE the view that inner city and other Urban Priority Area residents
need to be involved in many of the processes of decision making about
their communities. Many people in Urban Priority Areas still feel
alienated or isolated from actions taken in their neighbourhoods.

7.30   WE RECOMMEND that the City Council and others extend the
involvement in and influence of Urban Priority Area residents
in Inner City Projects.

Housing

7.31 THE COMMISSION IS DISMAYED at the continuing decline of the
state of the older housing stock in the City, and at the
difficulties in improving much of the inter-war and newer
stock of council housing. Much of the high rise housing developed in
response to the rehousing drive in the 1950s to 1970s has design faults
— some of which have led to structural defects affecting living
conditions. Chapter 5 section (d) (paras. 5.37 to 5.53) sets out the
details. It is vitally important that decent housing is available for all —
it is fundamental to health and wellbeing. Resources need to be drawn
into improving housing by new approaches and partnerships, including
the involvement of local people, with the aim of improving the poorer
quality housing stock in both the public, private and voluntary sectors.
We have seen new approaches during our housing visits (see Chapter
5). Improved local estate management is welcomed by the Commission.
We are concerned that the human and physical costs of failure to
improve housing conditions grow annually. We are concerned also
about the possible effects of housing legislation on people in low income
households and on the ability of the local authority to continue to
provide for that need which others may not be able or willing to meet.
WE BELIEVE that the role of the local authority should not be reduced to
the provision of residual welfare housing.

7.32 WE RECOMMEND that central government allocates further
resources to the council housing repair system to make it more
responsive to tenants' needs.

7.33 WE URGE that the local authority continues to press central
government to make available adequate resources to ensure
that the dilapidated housing stock in Urban Priority Areas is
improved as quickly as possible.

7.34 WE RECOMMEND that the local authority and housing associations monitor and continue to review their housing allocations
and transfer procedures and policies, in order to ensure that
discrimination against ethnic minority people does not occur.

Economic Regeneration

7.35 Economic regeneration is about jobs, employment and the
economic health of Birmingham. It is also about the need to
expand the level of income generation and wealth. This

depends upon the efficiency, viability and competitiveness of firms in the Birmingham area and upon what happens nationally. Central government and the local authority each have a role to play as does the voluntary sector. WE AFFIRM the important role of Trades Unions in seeking to extend the economic development potential of the City.

7.36   WE COMMEND the present good relations between the City Council and the private sector, especially the Chamber of Commerce and the CBI, and urge that they continue to be developed. We encourage Trades Unions' participation in such developments. (See also recommendations 7.25 and 7.26.)

Education

7.37   Here we make a number of specific recommendations drawn from Chapter 5, section (e) (paras. 5.54 to 5.86). WE COMMEND the commitment of the teachers and officers we met, yet consider they need more support for the work that they are trying to do. WE URGE both central and local government to recognize the need to improve Birmingham's Education Service. The education service plays a vital part in the development of Birmingham's young citizens. There is an important partnership between parents, children and the community in education.

7.38   We draw to the City Council's attention the need to seek more adequate ways of managing teaching and other staff in the context of falling rolls, and of providing better mechanisms for suitable teacher cover for those on maternity leave, absence or in-service training. WE ARE CONCERNED that spending on teaching equipment, books and materials has been low over the last few years compared with other education authorities. This particularly affects children in Urban Priority Area schools. We believe that greater attention should be paid to the poor condition of some school buildings and their state of cleanliness. Conditions in some of the inner city areas are especially bad. It is our view that all schools should be given adequate opportunities to develop industrial, commercial, technical and practical education. We see industry, partly through industry/school 'compacts', as playing an important role, together with the education service, in this development.

7.39   WE RECOMMEND that the Local Education Authority reviews the level of teaching staff and ancillary support in Urban Priority Area schools in both inner and outer areas.

7.40   WE RECOMMEND that the Local Education Authority appoints a specialist adviser with exclusive responsibility for Religious Education.

7.41   WE RECOMMEND that headteachers encourage parents and others from ethnic minority communities to seek election to the governing bodies of schools. We wish to encourage appropriate training for school governors.

7.42   WE RECOMMEND that the Local Education Authority ensures that good multi-cultural educational practice should be extended to all schools whether or not they are in ethnically mixed areas. This should be accompanied by a recognition that schools have an important role to play in anti-racist education.

7.43   WE RECOMMEND that the issues of community use and dual use of schools be reviewed by the City Council with a view to providing an effective integrated service. We believe that this review should be undertaken in parallel with the introduction of a firm policy of community education by the Local Education Authority. These matters are particularly important in Urban Priority Areas.

Poverty and Low Income

7.44   Urban Priority Areas as zones of multiple deprivation are characterized by low incomes and poverty. Unemployment is relatively high and many are supported by state benefits. A wide range of agencies are involved in alleviating poverty. The local authority plays an important role through housing rebates and allowances; social services and voluntary advice centres provide help; initiatives for the unemployed including training programmes are available. Family breakdown and problems of debt are significant. The problems are complex and many agencies are involved. The role of central government in many of these programmes is vital (see Chapter 5 sections (b) and (d) (paras. 5.2 to 5.18 and 5.37 to 5.53). WE ARE CONCERNED that income maintenance policies should enable people in poverty, without stigma, to have resources to improve their self-esteem. We reflect considerable concern in the City about the introduction of the 1988 Social Fund and would urge the local authority and others to keep its operation under review.

7.45   WE RECOMMEND that, as the growth of household debt is now a very serious contributory cause of social problems, the

Birmingham Voluntary Service Council should meet urgently with agencies involved in debt counselling, and credit unions, to develop an agreed strategy in the City to cope with this problem. We urge bankers, finance houses, loan companies, retailers, the local authority, the voluntary sector and others to seek to develop a pattern of alternative and sensitive lending mechanisms and revised debt collection practices along money advice lines.

Leisure and Recreation

7.46   WE COMMEND the local authority's approach to charging and fee levels for lower income groups. Access to leisure and recreation facilities in Urban Priority Areas should not be hindered by language, culture or price. In Urban Priority Areas young people lack appropriate leisure and recreation facilities locally. Such facilities are seen by local people as very important. The private and voluntary sectors as well as the local authority have important provision and management roles to play. We note the need to introduce further measures to enhance the community development function across the departments of the local authority in conjunction with the voluntary sector, local communities and groups.

7.47   WE RECOMMEND that the City Council should review the accessibility of leisure and recreational facilities to people in Urban Priority Areas. It would need to consider types of facility and local demand and needs. We feel there is benefit in linking some of the provision to school sites and other community use sites. (See also recommendation 7.43.)

7.48   WE RECOMMEND that the City Council, through all relevant departments and the voluntary sector, undertakes a review to ascertain the most effective method of co-ordinating its community development function.

Social Care

7.49   Social care facilities are vital to the wellbeing of many of those people least able to care for themselves. Relatives, friends and neighbours play important roles as informal carers in the City, while churches and voluntary groups provide many facilities. The local authority has various statutory duties in relation to the many social services client groups (see Chapter 5 section (f) paras. 5.87 to 5.97).

Clearly any adequate strategy for social care must rely on a multiplicity of individuals and agencies. We welcome the attention which has recently been given to services for the mentally ill and mentally handicapped, and we urge that this work be further developed. WE COMMEND moves by the City Council to decentralize services. We see this as a useful means of encouraging greater accessibility for the public, and of providing a range of services concerned with social care and other matters e.g. housing. Neighbourhood offices and area sub-committees should be encouraged to play a greater part in co-ordinating action in communities alongside the voluntary sector.

7.50 WE RECOMMEND that the City Council, health authorities and others consider the adequate and proper implementation of care within the community programmes. For elderly people, mentally ill people, physically handicapped people and others a major stumbling block has been the inadequate financing of care in the community programmes and the sometimes difficult issues of inter-agency collaboration in individual cases.

7.51 WE RECOMMEND that the City Council, through its relevant departments and the voluntary sector jointly undertake a review of service provision for the under 5 year olds in the light of the chronic underprovision in Urban Priority Areas in particular.

Health and Medical Care

7.52 The health of people in the inner city and in other Urban Priority Areas is poorer than that of the more affluent. (See Chapter 5, section (i) paras. 5.126 to 5.136). Lack of money and poor physical surroundings make people more vulnerable to illness and to the social burdens which illness imposes. Such people are highly dependent on the provisions of the National Health Service and social services and can rarely opt into the private medical sector for help. WE URGE the need for sufficient funding of the Area Health Authorities to enable them to provide adequate hospital facilities to reduce dangerously long waiting lists, and to respond properly to the trend towards increased care within the community of the elderly, chronically sick, mentally ill, mentally handicapped and the physically disabled. We welcome the Griffiths and Wagner Reports. (See recommendation 7.50.) WE WISH TO ENCOURAGE improvements in the quality of primary medical care, including the placing of professional skills within the community, in order to develop a greater sensitivity to the local needs of Urban Priority Areas. In particular we encourage further work in improving the senstitivity of the health and medical services to the needs of ethnic minority groups.

7.53   WE RECOMMEND that the Regional and Area Health Authorities give more attention to preventive medicine in Urban Priority Areas. We believe that Urban Priority Area residents lag behind in health education terms but have proportionately more to gain from preventive measures. Such measures need the active support of other agencies.

Order and Law

7.54   In some Urban Priority Areas the police are working alongside other agencies and are contributing to improving the quality of life through reduced vandalism, greater security, general youth work and community liaison. Residents have told us that improved home and locality security is an important factor for many individuals and communities. Many residents are appreciative of this work. We recognize that the police often have a difficult task in enforcing order and law.

7.55   WE COMMEND the efforts of the Police Force in its policy of recruitment from ethnic minority groups and are encouraged by the latest recruitment figures; we stress the need for police officers to be given adequate understanding of different cultures, racism and styles of life within the City. WE ALSO COMMEND the police for work done with local people on a number of Urban Priority Area estates and with local community projects. We are concerned by the increasing violence being used against the police. We are concerned by the evidence that, in spite of the work of Policy Consultative Committees, some residents of Urban Priority Areas and especially black people do not believe that their representations are being listened to or acted upon.

7.56   WE RECOMMEND that an independent study be undertaken of the work of Police Consultative Committees, with particular reference to the creating of conditions in which the voice of Urban Priority Area people can be effectively heard. WE RECOMMEND that the Birmingham Council of Christian Churches explore means to this end.

7.57   WE RECOMMEND that the Home Office should provide for a higher establishment of police officers in the West Midlands.

7.58   WE RECOMMEND that the West Midlands Police Force continues to give attention to monitoring racial attitudes amongst officers and to develop appropriate racial awareness amongst officers. WE RECOMMEND that outside bodies, including the churches, leaders of ethnic minority communities and others be actively involved in police training at all levels.

7.59   WE RECOMMEND that the Police Authority should give greater prominence to police work in the area of crime prevention, involving other appropriate agencies and individuals.

Voluntary Sector

7.60   A wide variety of flourishing voluntary bodies is one of the first essentials of a free democratic society. Their role is not auxiliary to statutory agencies, but fundamental to their healthy functioning. In this report we are dealing with voluntary societies which have arisen out of a need expressed by particular sections of the community either to urge action on issues such as housing, and the delivery of medical services, or to provide a service for members of the community such as a club for disabled children or a visiting service for the elderly. Voluntary organizations are an important integral part of the Birmingham community. In some cases innovative work by the voluntary sector leads to services being taken up and developed by statutory authorities, in others they provide an ongoing complement or supplement to statutory work. As work and services develop, a stage is reached by many organizations where their continued existence depends on the employment of paid staff. This is particularly true where professional services are being provided — this does not alter the voluntary nature of the organization which remains non-statutory.

7.61   The City's voluntary sector is complex and ever changing. Christian organizations and bodies representing other living faith communities are active at the local and city-wide levels. The Birmingham Community Relations Council, the Birmingham Voluntary Services Council, the Birmingham Council of Christian Churches and the Birmingham Council for Voluntary Youth Services are the major city-wide umbrella bodies with salaried staff and secretariats which bring the voluntary organizations together. There are others with a more specific remit like meetings of housing associations, the Birmingham Interfaiths Council, the groupings of money advice centres and the Standing Conference on Single Homeless. At local level also some umbrella organizations exist e.g. the Summerfield Project and Councils of Churches. Church organizations as well as individual Christians play an active part in many of these organizations. THE COMMISSION WISHES TO AFFIRM this form of Christian service.

7.62   WE RECOMMEND a thorough review of the role, organization and funding of the voluntary sector in Birmingham by the local authority in conjunction with the four major bodies mentioned in para. 7.61. This should note the work on grant aid by the Birmingham Voluntary Services Council and concern over Social Services Department's policy to the voluntary sector.

7.63   WE RECOMMEND that the voluntary sector through its four principal umbrella bodies positively seek out new ways of funding for the future e.g. from commerce and industry.

7.64   WE RECOMMEND that the City Council and the four major voluntary umbrella bodies take action to develop and sustain voluntary sector activity in middle ring and outer council estates. These outer Urban Priority Areas have great difficulty in obtaining funding. This requires review and action by the voluntary sector, the local authority and others.

Conclusions

7.65   In the midst of great cities there is squalor and poverty. The division into separate, often adjacent, areas of comfortable and deprived Birmingham must provoke profound questions about our City and our individual lives. Advocates of the 'civic gospel' encouraged Joseph Chamberlain and city leaders in their task of developing a Birmingham of practical justice and social care rooted in religious idealism. We stand in this inheritance and believe that we must speak.

7.66   Throughout this Report we have examined the structures, policies and practice of a range of bodies which affect the lives of those who live in Urban Priority Areas. Many of us are members of those powerful bodies and must seek to speed up the often slow delivery of greater prosperity and status to those who live in Urban Priority Areas. We must guard against becoming obstacles to a proper priority being given to the needs of Urban Priority Areas.

7.67   We declare as Christians that the status and value of people does not ultimately depend upon their success or prosperity. Despite all efforts some will continue to be deprived. A loving concern and person to person care for any who remain deprived will always be an obligation on all human beings. Such an attitude and relationship is a reflection of the dignity of all people as the children of God.

7.68 Our conclusions and recommendations aim at encouraging actions which will bind all the citizens of Birmingham together in sharing the fruits of recovery from recession. We have faith in the City of Birmingham and its people as being equal to that task. This will demand a concentration of imagination and resources on Urban Priority Areas. There are tough human and economic issues facing the City. We have attempted to describe and highlight them. They are problems and opportunities for us all, not only for the disadvantaged. There is little likelihood that 'somehow' prosperity will 'trickle down' to the disadvantaged and that urban decay will disappear without determined planning and direction of economic and social resources. Commitment to the healing both of economic and of social wounds is demanded if faith is to be kept with the City of Birmingham and all its people. If these tasks are grasped we shall be building upon a faith that proclaims all people as sharers in the goodness of all that is created.

7.69 Such a proclamation invites a response.

Appendixes

Appendix A

(1) *List of those who have contributed or submitted evidence to the Commission*

Director of Social Services
City Treasurer
City Housing Officer
Director of Environmental Services
Director of Recreation and Community Services
Head of the Race Relations and Equal Opportunities Unit
Director of Education
Director of Development

Birmingham City Council

Birmingham Anglican Diocesan Council for Social Responsibility
West Midlands Probation Service
DHSS (Midlands Region)
South Birmingham Health Authority
Central Birmingham Health Authority
Birmingham Credit Union Development Agency Ltd
Aston University
Balsall Heath Community Association
Birmingham Council of Voluntary Youth Services
Engineering Employers West Midlands Association
West Midlands Council for Sport and Recreation
Westhill College
Afro-Caribbean Trading Unit (Multicultural Support Service)
Handsworth Breakthrough Trust
Birmingham Churches Managing Agency
Birmingham Baptist Inner City Project
Dr. Jorgen Nielsen (Centre for the Study of Islam and Christian — Muslim relations)
Revd. Richard Bashford (Greenspring Training Scheme)
Revd. N. Power, Vicar of Ladywood
Canon Tom Walker (St. John and St. Germain)
Revd. Dr. Bellamy (Chaplain — Queen Elizabeth Hospital)
Revd. Dr. I. M. Kenway (St. Mary and St. John, Alum Rock)
Revd. David Horn (St. James' Aston)
Revd. R. D. Hindley (St. Chad's, Erdington)
St. Cuthbert's Neighbourhood Youth and Community Centre
Churches Industrial Group, Birmingham
St. Basil's Centre
Birmingham Inter-Faiths Council

John Russell (Diocesan Committee for Relations with People of Other Faiths)
Roger Hooker (Church of the Ascension — Sikh Community input)
Revd. Robert Morris (Parish of St. James)
Revd. Michael Hutchinson (Society of Friends)
Revd. Des Pemberton (Wesleyan Holiness)
Revd. D. Lambelle (Elim Churches)
Revd. C. Hughes Smith (Free Churches)
Revd. J. Waller (United Reformed Church)
Revd. P. Loveitt (United Reformed Church)
Revd. P. Walker (Baptist)
Revd. N. B. Hall (Baptist)
Birmingham Settlement
Confederation of British Industry
West Midlands Police
Birmingham Council of Christian Churches
Birmingham Community Forum
Mr. B. W. Tanner, Deputy Chairman of Conservative Association
Reverend Rajinder K. Daniel, Diocesan Adviser on Black Affairs
Ian Bennett, Diocesan Training Officer, Advisory Council for Training
    Birmingham Diocese
Canon Tompkins, Handsworth
Laurie Green (Principal — Aston Training Scheme)
Mr. J. Heaton, 126 Westfield Road

(2) *Visits by the Commission*

Adullam Homes
Aston Residents' Association
Baverstock School, Druids Heath
Birmingham Chamber of Industry and Commerce
Birmingham Diocesan Council for Social Responsibility
Birmingham City Council Environmental Services Department and site visits
Birmingham City Council Housing Department and site visits
Birmingham City Council Race Relations Unit
Birmingham City Council Recreation and Community Services Department,
    Ladywood Area Office
Birmingham City Council Urban Renewal Area Office, Aston
Birmingham Community Forum
Black Business in Birmingham
Confederation of British Industry
Golden Croft Warden Scheme, Handsworth
Handsworth and Aston Forum of Churches
Holte School, Aston
Olive Branch Community Centre
Representatives of Various Ethnic Minority Associations
Sikh Youth Service
Springhill Community Centre
West Midlands Police
Wyrley Birch Estate Tenants Association

Appendix B

FURTHER READING

This is a list of some publications which readers of our Report may find helpful for further study.

Archbishop of Canterbury's Commission on Urban Priority Areas, *Faith in the city*, Church House Publishing, London, 1985.

Birmingham City Council, *Independent inquiry into the Handsworth disturbances*, Report of a Committee of Inquiry, Birmingham, 1986.

A. Briggs, *A history of Birmingham 1865–1938*, vol. 2, Oxford University Press, Oxford, 1952.

Central Birmingham Health Authority, *A picture of health?*, Annual Report, Birmingham, 1987.

L. Green, *Power to the powerless: theology brought to life*, Marshall Pickering, Basingstoke, 1987.

H. M. Government, *Action for cities*, HMSO, London, 1988.

H. M. Government, Birmingham City Council, Birmingham District Health Authorities, *Birmingham Inner City Partnership, Annual Review*, 1987.

K. Spencer et al, *Crisis in the industrial heartland: a study of the West Midlands*, Oxford University Press, Oxford, 1986.

A. Sutcliffe and R. Smith, *Birmingham, 1939–1970*, Oxford University Press, Oxford, 1974.

West Midlands County Council, *A different reality*, Report of a Review Panel on the Lozells Disturbances of 1985, Birmingham, 1986.

Maps

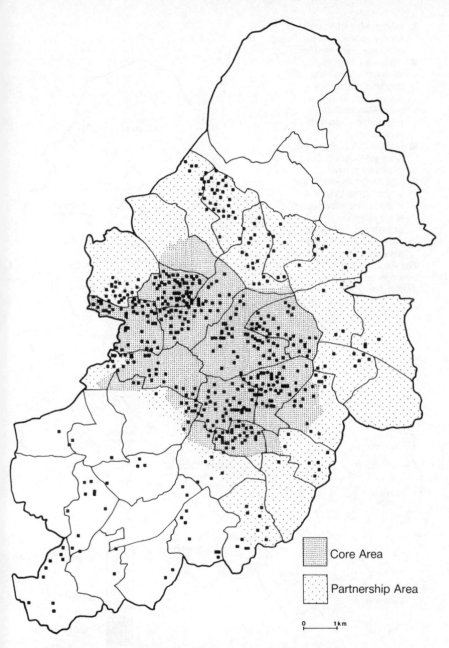

MAP 1.1 Birmingham Core Area and Partnership Area
showing the location of Enumeration Districts falling within the worst 10% in
England and Wales 1981

Core Area

Partnership Area

0   1 km

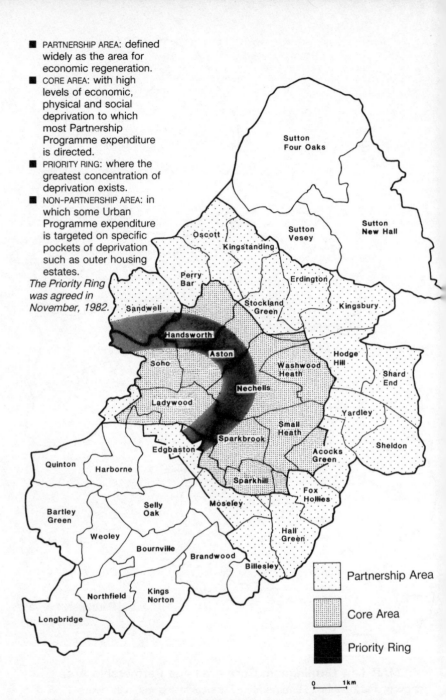

- ■ PARTNERSHIP AREA: defined widely as the area for economic regeneration.
- ■ CORE AREA: with high levels of economic, physical and social deprivation to which most Partnership Programme expenditure is directed.
- ■ PRIORITY RING: where the greatest concentration of deprivation exists.
- ■ NON-PARTNERSHIP AREA: in which some Urban Programme expenditure is targeted on specific pockets of deprivation such as outer housing estates.

The Priority Ring was agreed in November, 1982.

Partnership Area

Core Area

Priority Ring

0   1km

MAP 1.2   Birmingham Electoral Wards and Area Definitions

158